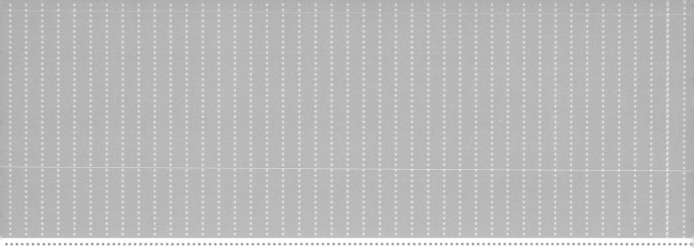

LITTLE CAKES

····· from the ·····

whimsical bakehouse

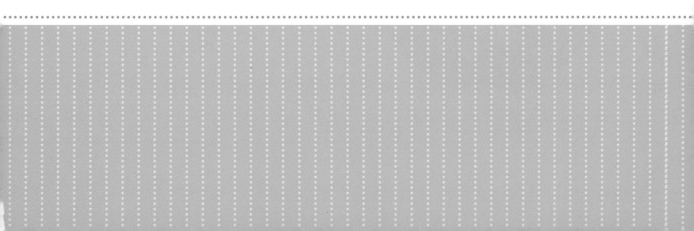

LITTLE CAKES

····· from the ·····

whimsical bakehouse

kaye hansen & liv hansen

PHOTOGRAPHS BY BEN FINK

Clarkson Potter/Publishers
New York

Copyright © 2008 by Liv Hansen and Kaye Hansen

All rights reserved.
Published in the United States by Clarkson Potter/Publishers, an imprint of the Crown Publishing Group, a division of Random House, Inc., New York.
www.crownpublishing.com
www.clarksonpotter.com

Clarkson N. Potter is a trademark and Potter and colophon are registered trademarks of Random House, Inc.

Library of Congress Cataloging-in-Publication Data
Hansen, Kaye.
    Little cakes from the Whimsical Bakehouse / Liv Hansen and Kaye Hansen; photographs by Ben Fink.
        p.   cm.
    Includes index.
    1. Cupcakes.   2. Muffins.   3. Cake.
I. Hansen, Liv.   II. Title.
TX771.H2845   2008
641.8'653—dc22   2007010069

ISBN 978-0-307-38282-5

Printed in the United States of America

Design by Laura Palese
Photographs by Ben Fink

10   9   8   7   6   5   4   3   2

First Edition

For KASE,
our best little one

a c k n o w l e d g m e n t s

Wow, round three. To everyone who found inspiration in our first two books, thank you. Without you our little cakes would not have been baked and decorated. Our home testers and Bakehouse members—Jaime Raucci, Mariana Cintron, Sara Romeo, Traci Sherman, and Jessica DiPaci—thank you for giving us peace of mind. Laura Palese, thank you for your spooky inspirations. And of course what would we do without the usual suspects, Carla Glasser, Ben Fink, Aliza Fogelson, and the Bakehouse staff and customers?

contents

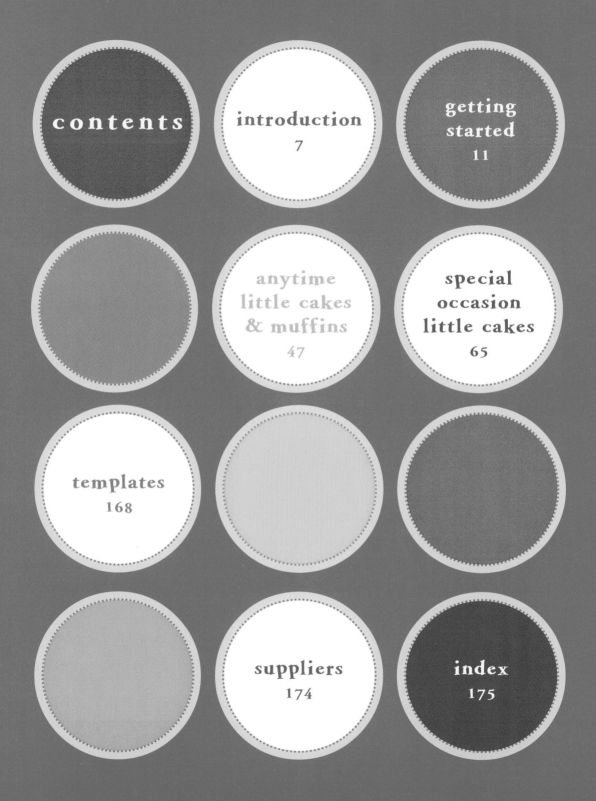

introduction

What is the allure of little cakes? Are they reminiscent of the magical tea parties we delighted in when we were small and the world seemed so big? Like chocolate, do they comfort our soul? Whether or not it's the child inside us that creates the appetite for these diminutive cakes, let's hope it stays, because little cakes are fun to make and fun to eat. After all, we all need a bit, and a bite, of joy in our lives.

Since the beginning of my decorating career, I have been fascinated with all things small. Even though I have been assisting my mom, Kaye, making her buttercream roses since I was ten, I didn't start experimenting with icing and chocolate until she opened up the Riviera Bakehouse in 1994, and we started our collaboration. My first decorating efforts graced the tops of cupcakes, an easy place to start for the novice. I covered them with piped buttercream spirals, polka dots, and stars in a festive palette. The first holiday I worked at the bakery was Halloween, and when we tested these simple though colorful treats with the public, they were a hit. Now our Halloween cupcakes go far beyond their simple roots, and although we still make some of the "old-fashioned" kind, each year I create new designs to delight our customers.

These days you may have noticed that cupcakes are BIG. Not just in size, although the Bakehouse does make a large cake that is decorated to look like a giant cupcake, but big in that they are ubiquitous. And we can't help ourselves; we love them too, not just the classic vanilla but carrot, lemon poppy, and caramel. These little gems are versatile; you can add dimension by applying chocolate decorations or go for a bit of trompe l'oeil by making the top look like a blooming rose or a basket. The options seem endless.

But your exploration of baking and decorating small cakes does not have to begin and end with cupcakes. My first foray into the world of miniature delights was not a petit four, but a four-inch chocolate cake that I baked and iced in bright sorbet colors and decorated with colored polka dots. My mom and I named it the Spring Fling. Ten years later we still make it. You, too, can find inspiration in the wide range of small cake pans that are on the market today, from 6-inch round cake pans right down to 2-inch round pans, from standard to mini muffin tins, from miniature Bundt to individual cheesecake pans. And as for 3-D or shaped pans, wow, I have found hemispheres, squares, cones, roses, sunflowers, ghosts, eggs, ice cream cones, hearts, bears, trains, wedding cakes, and more. Most of the time, just baking in one of these specialty molds will yield a cake that is pleasing to the eye. Add a little color, a dab of buttercream, a drizzle of chocolate, or a dusting of confectioners' sugar and voilà! Of course, most of the time I let my whimsical side run rampant, and before I know it, what was once a simple cone has become a witch's hat, a Christmas tree, or a shark breaching the water's surface.

Although the recipes in this book were baked in small pans, they can be baked in standard round or sheet pans as well. In fact many of these recipes come from the stock cake collection at our bakery. Whenever we whip up a batch of cheesecakes we bake most of the batter in our standard 7-inch round pans but we also set some aside to bake in individual-size ramekins. In this book we bake our Red Velvet cake in a small cone pan and decorate it to look like a shark, but we also use this recipe at the bakery to make the classic Red Velvet cake iced with Kids' Buttercream. So don't feel limited by size or flavor. We encourage you to mix and match recipes and designs. If Caramel Cake is your favorite but you have your heart set on making Basket Cupcakes, just switch recipes, adjusting the amount of batter or icing accordingly. For the most part, all of the recipes are interchangeable, with the possible exception of the cheesecakes, meringues, cream puffs, and truffles, which don't lend themselves to being baked in shaped pans, or to being filled or sculpted.

Because little cakes are lighthearted, it is often hard to take them seriously. Without a doubt there will be a sense of whimsy, but we'll also show you how a few simple touches transform little cakes into delicate and beautiful desserts. Take the Bakehouse's signature Mini Birthday Cake as an example. It is decorated with six bright colors, piped swags, borders, and edible candles . . . to say the least, it is an eye catcher. But erase the neon palette and you could be looking at a tier of a traditional wedding cake. Instead of using vivid colors, choose a softer palette, tone on tone, or all white. Instead of overpowering the presentation with too much decoration, keep it simple. Long the staple of kids' birthday parties, cupcakes are breaking free from their bonds. Now brides and grooms clamor to get their hands on them, too. On page 131 we will show you how to tier your cupcakes on stacked cake pedestals—perfect for a wedding.

The decorating process does not have to be daunting; in fact, a simple but creative presentation will add panache to little cakes. Fortunately, my mom's wonderful recipes are tasty enough to satisfy anyone. By serving the Pistachio Ganache Truffles in a pool of Caramel Sauce on a beautiful plate, you can set a seductive mood. Or by arranging your cupcakes on stacked pedestal cake plates or a wire pastry tree you are creating a playful centerpiece. Throughout the book we will give decorating, plating, and arranging tips to help you create the aura you want.

The level of difficulty of the sweets and the decorations ranges from simple to advanced, and will be noted in the recipe title, from one star, indicating a recipe or design that is easy to make or decorate, up to three stars for a challenging cake. Whenever possible we will offer alternatives to simplify the designs (see Simple Decorating Tips, page 37). Most recipes can stand on their own without decoration, while others deserve to be over the top. Explore and see which recipes and designs bring a smile to your face and a grumble of anticipation to your belly, and then go for it. My mom and I both love the thrill of trying something new, whether it is a recipe or a decorating technique, and even more we love seeing the delighted reaction of our customers and coworkers. Or why not create just for your own fulfillment? After all, what is more whimsical than a miniature cake just for you—one you don't have to share. We hope you find inspiration within these pages to venture out into new territory.

—Liv Hansen

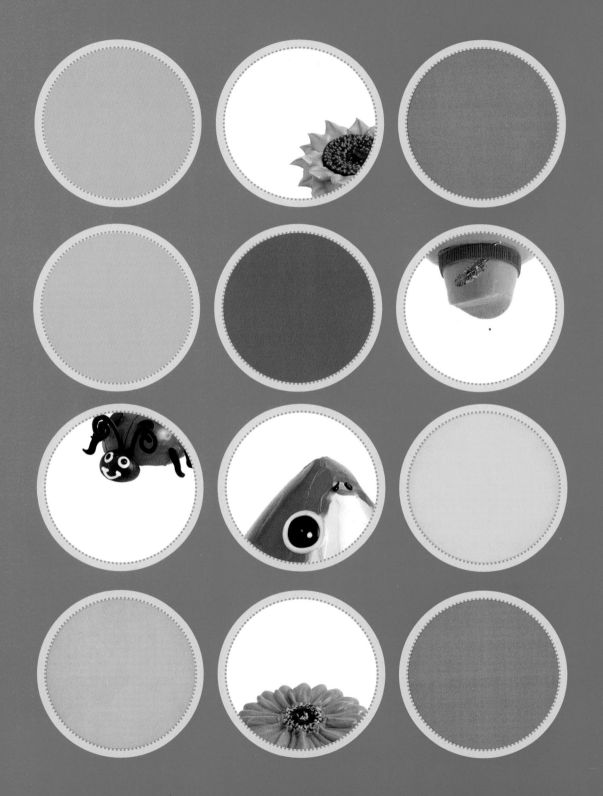

GETTING STARTED

If you are like me, you probably want to dive in and tackle a recipe or design.

I am known for decorating cakes on a whim with little planning and a lot of surprise results. Luckily I am often rewarded with beautiful or kooky cakes, but that's after a long road of trial and error, from which I learn from mistakes and, through experimentation, discover new ways of decorating. Even if you are a bit impatient to get started, I recommend reading through this chapter. It contains invaluable information on tools of the trade, helpful baking and decorating tips, tricks for assembling little cakes, icing recipes, and hints for working with chocolate and decorating techniques that appear throughout the book.

tools of the trade

Here is a list of the basic tools you need to bake and decorate little cakes. Included is a chart to help you sort through the multitude of baking pans we used in this book.

Tools for Baking and Decorating

- **Bases**—Every dessert, from the lowly cupcake right up to a tiered wedding cake, needs something to be served on. It may be a napkin or it may be fine china. At the Bakehouse we cover cardboard rounds with decorative foil or doilies. It is easy, inexpensive, transportable, and disposable. Just make sure the base you choose fits the cake you plan on making. Ideally the base, whether it is a cake plate, cardboard round, or dessert plate, is sturdy and flat and at least 2 inches larger than the cake itself.

  - **Cardboard**—Even little cakes need a stable base for assemblage and presentation. Cardboard rounds make it easier to handle the cakes and give a clean edge for icing. You can purchase precut rounds in a variety of sizes; or, if you can't get your hands on the shape or size you need, trace your cake pan (or cake) onto a sheet of corrugated cardboard and cut it out with scissors. Cover cardboard rounds with decorative foil and you have a perfect portable and disposable base for your decorated cake.

  - **Cellophane**—At the Bakehouse we like to make our small pastry cones out of cellophane instead of parchment paper because they maintain a clean, sharp point as you work. We get 1.25 ml thick cellophane in precut 10" x 10" squares from our paper supplier. If you don't want to search the web for this product, you can buy cellophane by the roll at craft stores. Cut the roll of cellophane into 10-inch squares, and then cut these squares in half diagonally. With the hypotenuse, or longest side, of the triangle facing up, hold each of the two acute-angled points separately between your thumb and fingers. First curl the top right point downward, wrapping under itself until it lines up with the left side of the right angle. Hold this in place while you wrap the top left point down and around the back of the pastry cone until it lines up with the right side of the right angle. Adjust the cellophane with your thumbs inside and your pointer fingers outside until a sharp point forms. Tape close to the base to maintain the cone shape. Cellophane is also a great surface on which to pipe out chocolate decorations. Parchment will work fine as a substitute for making pastry cones and as a design work surface.

- **Cake pans**—See chart on pages 16–17.

- **Coupler and ring**—See Pastry bag, below.

- **Electric mixer**—This modern convenience is very handy; at the bakery, it is essential. Any brand will do, but we recommend the reliable 5-quart KitchenAid. With some elbow grease, most cake recipes can be made without the aid of an electric mixer. Handheld mixers also get the job done.

- **Metal spatula**—Metal spatulas come in all shapes and sizes. The small offset spatula (4½ inches), which we refer to at the Bakehouse as a "baby bent," is great for spreading icing on cupcakes or for any other small and delicate task. This may be the only spatula you need, but I find the 10-inch offset spatula useful for icing some of the "larger" cakes.

- **Muffin scoop**—We use muffin scoops, much like an ice cream scoop, to scoop muffin and cake batter into their small pans. Scoops are neat, and they evenly divide the batter, which allows for a consistent result. There are many scoops on the market; we recommend buying one with a spring-action lever that cleans out the inner shell of the scoop.

- **Paint brush**—Soft sable or acrylic brushes are used to paint with melted chocolate. For detailed shading I recommend using a #0, 1, or 2 brush.

- **Parchment paper**—This versatile paper is similar to wax paper, but without the wax coating. Use it to line cake pans to prevent baked goods from sticking. Chocolate doesn't stick to it, either, so any chocolate design, no matter how delicate, can be piped onto it. See Cellophane, above, for instructions for making a cone.

- **Pastry bag**—These cone-shaped bags make piping decorations a breeze. We recommend 12-inch polyester bags, which can be washed and reused. Disposable ones are available, but they are not as strong. The coupler, a plastic insert, allows you to change tips with ease. The ring screws on the outside of the bag and coupler to secure the tip in place. As an alternative, you can place a tip directly inside a bag without a coupler. Just make sure the hole is not too big, or the tip will slip right out. If you do not have a pastry bag handy, you can always make a pastry cone with parchment paper or cellophane (see Cellophane, above).

- **Pastry cones**—See Cellophane or Parchment paper, above.

- **Rubber spatula**—Like bowls or knives, a spatula is one of those items we find essential at the Bakehouse. Spatulas are perfect for scraping down your mixing bowl and mixing colors into buttercream or white wafer chocolate.

- **Scraper**—To ice a cake to a smooth finish, we often use a flat-edged metal or plastic scraper instead of a metal spatula. A bench scraper with a rolled handle can do the job as well. One side of the scraper rests flat on a turntable while the other edge runs flush with the cake, making for a steadier hand and a smooth finish. They are difficult to find, but if you decorate cakes often, it is worth the search.

- **Straws**—For the small-tiered cakes featured in this book, drinking straws are used to support the tiers. Drinking straws can also be used to make chocolate candles (see Adventurous Alternative, page 94).

- **Tips**—There is a special tip for almost every piping application. For a good selection of tips, I recommend buying a starter set. Tips can also be purchased individually. Before starting any design, make sure you have the appropriate tips. When applicable, I have noted alternative tips that can be used to achieve similar piping results. Check the suppliers listed on page 174 to order individual tips or sets.

- **Turntable**—Similar to a lazy Susan, a turntable makes icing a cake more efficient and neat. I use a heavy-duty metal turntable made by Ateco. They are expensive, but they're worth the money if you decorate cakes often.

- **Wire cooling rack**—These wire racks are used to cool cakes. We often place the pan itself on the rack to cool, rather than removing the hot cakes from their pans right away. They are also indispensable when glazing cakes or making chocolate molds.

Special Ingredients for Decorating

- **Food coloring**—We depend on liquid gel colors (a professional product) for achieving our vivid icing hues. They are sold at most high-end baking supply stores or through mail order. However, paste colors, which are more readily available, work just as well. Liquid colors, available at most grocery stores, can be used, but the palette is limited and they are less concentrated. For coloring the wafer chocolate, we use candy colors. These oil-based colors are used by confectioners to tint white chocolate; find them at candy-making specialty stores, craft stores, or from mail-order sources.

- **Sprinkles/nonpareils**—These are perfect for making any little cake festive and fun. You can even mix them into some cake batters to create a colorful confetti surprise.

- **Wafer chocolate**—Wafer chocolate is actually not chocolate; it is a candy coating also known as confectioners' chocolate. It is easier to work with than chocolate because it does not need to be tempered (so it stays shiny after it resolidifies). It comes in dark chocolate, white chocolate, and a limited range of colors. For more information on decorating with chocolate see pages 39—43.

Nowadays, miniature cake pans come in all different "little" shapes. In addition to cupcake pans and small cake pans, we have found many fun pans with shaped molds, from hearts to trains and from miniature Bundts to pans specially made for cheesecakes. In addition to the classic metal pans, and nonstick pans, many of the mini cake forms are now made out of nonstick silicone. We still prefer the metal or nonstick kind, because we found that cakes baked in silicone tend to burn more easily. But I did find a use for some of the silicone molds: they were great as chocolate molds.

Cake Pans	Pan Size	Mold Size	Batter Capacity	No. of Molds
MINI MUFFIN/ CUPCAKE	10" x 15"	1¾" across x 1" deep	1½ tablespoons	24
STANDARD MUFFIN/ CUPCAKE	7" x 11"	2¾" across x 1½" deep	¼ to ⅓ cup	6
	11" x 15"	2¾" across x 1½" deep	¼ to ⅓ cup	12
		2¾" across x 1½" deep	¼ to ⅓ cup	24
JUMBO (GIANT) MUFFIN	10" x 13½"	3¾" across x 1¾" deep	⅔ to ¾ cup	6
MINI ROSE PAN	12" round	2½" inch round	¼ cup	12
CONE PAN (MINI WONDER MOLD)	10" x 10"	3½" across x 3" deep	¾ cup	4
ICE CREAM CONE PAN	10" round	2¾" across x 3" deep	½ cup	6
MINI BOWL PAN	8" x 12"	3" across x 1½" deep	¼ to ⅓ cup	6
MINI TIERED PAN SET	4", 3", 2" round	2" deep	1 cup, ½ cup, ¼ cup	1 each
4-INCH ROUND	4" round	3" deep	1½ cups	1

Cake Pans	Pan Size	Mold Size	Batter Capacity	No. of Molds
6-INCH ROUND	6" round	3" deep	3 cups	1
SCALLOPED MINI HEART PAN	11½" x 15"	3¾" across x 3¾" deep	¾ cup	6
MINI SQUARE PAN	11" x 15"	2½" x 2½" x 1½" deep	½ cup	12
MINI CHEESECAKE PAN		2" across x 1½" deep	¼ cup	12
MINI HEART CHEESECAKE PAN	10½" x 14"	2" deep	¼ cup	12
PINEAPPLE UPSIDE DOWN	9½" x 12"	1½" deep	½ cup	6
MINI BUNDT PAN	9" x 13"	3¾" across x 1¾" deep	½ cup	6
TWINKIE PAN	9" x 13"	4½" across x 1½" deep	⅓ cup	8
SILICONE MUFFIN/ CUPCAKE LINERS	set of 6 or 12	2¾" across x 1½" deep	¼ to ⅓ cup	6 or 12
HALF-SHEET PAN	12" x 16"	12" x 16" x 1"	6 cups	1

baking tips

We hope these useful hints will help you bake even more
delicious goodies.

- It probably goes without saying, but please make sure you
have all of the ingredients and equipment you need before you
start a recipe. We also recommend familiarizing yourself with a
recipe by giving it a read through before you begin.

- Always remember to preheat your oven. This will help ensure that the cakes bake properly. Ideally have an oven thermometer to check the temperature. One of our cake testers was having difficulty getting the proper rising and baking times for some cakes when she discovered her oven was not the correct temperature.

- Carefully measure all of your ingredients because baking is a science; it requires accuracy.

- Unless otherwise noted, it is important to have your ingredients, especially your butter and eggs, at room temperature. This will facilitate the creaming and mixing process.

- Unless otherwise noted, use a paddle attachment for combining ingredients in an electric mixer.

- Always remember to scrape down your mixing bowl often with a spatula, being careful to get all the way to the bottom of the bowl where sometimes the paddle or whip does not reach. This will ensure that all of the ingredients are well combined.

- If you don't have enough pans to bake all of your little cakes at once, use just one pan and bake in batches. Since the baking times are so short, the batter can be left at room temperature. Meringues, however, cannot sit out; they must be baked immediately.

- Most cakes have a rather short shelf life: only 2 to 5 days in an airtight container in the refrigerator or from 2 to 3 days at room temperature. But most cakes can be frozen after baking. We always store our unassembled and undecorated cakes and cupcakes in the freezer. Keeping them chilled makes them less likely to crumble and fall apart during decorating. Once they have cooled, wrap in plastic wrap and, if sealed well, they can last up to 1 month in the freezer. To thaw, place the cake, still wrapped, in the refrigerator overnight. Remove from the refrigerator when you are ready to assemble or ice. Alternatively, take the cake out of the freezer, still wrapped, and let it sit for 5 minutes (approximate time for a cupcake) to 30 minutes (approximate time for a 6-inch round), depending on the size. So if you know you will be short on time later, bake your cakes now, freeze, and assemble or decorate them the day you need them, or even the day before.

- Bundt cakes and pound cakes can be made in advance. Simply pour the batter into the pregreased pan or pans you plan on baking in. Wrap in plastic wrap and store in the refrigerator for up to 2 days or in the freezer for up to a month (or more if the wrapping is airtight). Simply remove from the refrigerator or freezer and let come to room temperature before baking.

- If you plan on serving your cakes a day or more after they are baked/decorated, or if it is a very hot day, chill the cakes until 1 to 4 hours before serving. For the fullest flavor, we recommend serving our little cakes at room temperature. In warmer weather, it will take less time for your cake to reach room temperature, but cakes iced in buttercream, as long as they are not in direct sunlight, can still be taken out of the refrigerator hours before serving. In cold weather you can leave a cake out anywhere from 3 hours to all day. Once a cake has come to room temperature try not to move it, because the layers might shift, and the design might break.

- Most cake and muffin recipes can be baked in cupcake papers.

- Never over-mix muffin or quick bread batters.

- Muffin batter or quick bread batters can be made up to 1 week ahead and stored in the refrigerator in an airtight container. Just scoop and bake whenever you want the aroma of freshly baked muffins to fill the air.

- We recommend using a muffin scoop, one with a spring-action lever, for scooping muffin and cake batter into their small molds. Not only is it neater, but you can divide the batter evenly.

- It is helpful to have a small ounce scale in the kitchen. It facilitates the measuring of chocolate, nuts, and other ingredients that are sold in ounces.

Notes on Baking Ingredients

- **Butter**—In our opinion, for taste purposes, butter is always superior to shortening or oil. But some of our muffin and icing recipes do call for the substitutes. When baking, use unsalted butter and unless otherwise noted, work with your butter at room temperature.

- **Kosher salt**—We use kosher salt at the bakery but table salt can be substituted measure for measure.

- **Pure vanilla extract**—For me there is no substitute for pure vanilla extract. The artificial extracts often leave a perfumed taste in your mouth.

- **High-ratio shortening**—A specialty product for bakers, high-ratio shortening contains emulsifiers that allow it to remain stable at a wider range of temperatures and enable it to hold more air when beaten, making icings fluffier. It can also incorporate more sugar and liquid than regular shortening without breaking, and it accepts coloring agents better. You can purchase this product through baking wholesalers (under the name Quick Blend) and on the web, from suppliers like countrykitchensa.com and cookscakeandcandy.com. Home use brand names include Alpine Hi-Ratio shortening and Sweetex. If you cannot get this product, however, the results you'll get with regular shortening will be fine.

- **Chocolate**—Most of the chocolate we bake with is either semisweet chocolate or cocoa powder. We use Dutch processed cocoa powder at the bakery as opposed to regular (Hershey's) cocoa powder. *Hershey's cocoa powder is good for Red Velvet cake, because its acidity creates a redder final product versus the darker chocolaty color of Dutch cocoa.* You can buy semisweet chocolate at the grocery store. It is normally sold in a break-apart tablet that is calibrated in ounces. This makes it easy to measure out the chocolate for your recipes.

filling, crumbing, & icing
LITTLE CAKES & CUPCAKES

In our first book, we filled and iced all of our cakes in the same manner. We approached all the little cakes in this book differently. To address these variations we have broken down this section into three parts: Filling, Crumbing, and Icing. But first there are some things you should know before working with any of the cakes.

- Never work with a warm cake, because it will crumble easily and melt the icing. Chilling the cake in the refrigerator for a few hours or overnight makes it much easier to work with. More often than not, we work with our cupcakes directly from the freezer. They defrost so quickly that by the time it comes to decorating them they have already partially or totally thawed. You can also wrap a cooled cake tightly in plastic wrap and freeze it for up to 1 month, letting it thaw when ready to use.

- If you plan on filling your creation, to ensure stability, your fillings should be as stiff as possible.

- Buttercream is the most stable of our icings. It holds up well under most weather conditions, unlike whipped cream, and acts as a protective shell, keeping the cake and filling fresh.

- Most muffins and cupcakes are served in their own paper liners. Other cakes need a base from which to serve them. This base could be a plate, a cupcake tree, or a cardboard round. Whatever the base, make sure it is large enough and strong enough to support and complete your cake with the decorations you have envisioned.

FILLING

Filling a Cupcake

It is an unexpected delight when you bite into a cupcake and discover a filling, even if it is just a morsel of mousse. You can tackle the task of filling a cupcake a few different ways. For each technique listed below, first remove the cupcakes from the freezer or refrigerator and let them come to room temperature.

1. The easiest way to fill a cupcake is to slice the top off of any cake that rises above the paper liner, pipe a giant swirl of mousse on the bottom, and replace the top. It won't resemble a cupcake anymore but it will definitely be delicious. If you want to ice the cupcake, simply pipe more mousse or icing on top.

2. A more discreet way to fill a cupcake is to slice the top off of the cupcake and set it aside. With a melon baller, or a small paring knife, scoop out a 1-inch-deep by 1-inch-wide cavity from the center of the cupcake; discard or snack on this piece. Fill this cavity with whatever filling you desire and replace the top. Chill for 15 minutes to 1 hour before icing and/or decorating.

3. The final option is the most amazing, but it will only work with light cakes, not dense cakes such as pound cake. Place the filling in a pastry bag with a coupler. Attach a round tip (#8, 9, or 10). Insert the tip of the pastry bag into the top of the cupcake and squeeze.* Continue squeezing until the filling just begins to seep out around the tip's edge. You will actually feel the cupcake expand in your hands as it fills. If desired, insert the tip again into another spot, being sure to stay at least ½ inch from the side of the cupcake.

To fill Cream Puffs, Nostalgic Nibbles, and Devilish Delights, follow the directions from step 3, but instead of inserting the pastry tip into the top, invert the pastry and insert the tip into the underside. This will keep the top surface unblemished.

Filling a Cake

It is quite simple to fill a little cake. Because the layers of cake are so small and the filling layers are so thin, there is no need to "ring the cake" as we do with our large cakes.

1. Let the cakes cool completely; preferably chill them for a few hours.

2. Start by leveling the cakes. Most cakes form a rounded dome when they are baked, so you will need to level the tops. Use a serrated knife and, keeping the knife horizontal, use a sawing action to cut off the rounded portions.

3. Cut the cakes into 3 layers (we recommend anywhere from two to four layers from one cake). To cut even layers, place the cake on a turntable. Rotate the turntable, lightly scoring the cake with a serrated knife at the place where it is to be cut in halves or thirds. Make sure the cut line is level and divides the cake equally. With your hand lightly resting on the cake to hold it steady, rotate the turntable as you use a sawing action to cut the cake along the guideline.

4. Adhere the bottom layer of the cake to the center of a cardboard round (or a portable base) with a drop of buttercream if you like. If the cake protrudes over the cardboard, trim the sides; but it should be no more than ⅛ inch from the cardboard edge.

5. Carefully set aside the top two layers of the cake. Spread half of the filling evenly over the first layer. The filling should be thin, no thicker than ¼ inch, and within the bounds of the cake's edge. This will make it easier to crumb-coat the cake.

6. Place the second layer of cake on top of the first, making sure it is centered and level. Spread the remaining filling on top of this layer. Place the final layer of cake on top, pressing gently with your hand to level the cake.

CRUMBING

Crumbing is the process of sealing an entire cake with a thin coating of icing. This "crumb coat" traps any stray or excess crumbs, sealing them in, thus creating a smooth backdrop for piped, spread, and applied decorations. Once chilled, this layer will also prevent crumbs from appearing in your final coat of icing.

Cupcakes in general do not need to be crumbed because they are not sliced. Even the filled ones usually have at most a few crumbs because the tops are replaced, sealing in any potential mess. On the other hand, cakes that are sliced and/or filled will generally need to be crumbed.

Crumbing a Cake

In nearly every case, you should use the same icing to crumb the cake that you will use to finish it. If you are planning on finishing with a color, however, your cake should be crumbed with uncolored buttercream, so don't tint your buttercream until you are ready to apply the finishing touches.

1. Place the filled cake in the center of the turntable.

2. Place a small amount of icing on top of the cake. With a metal spatula, spread the icing evenly over the entire top of the cake, making it as smooth as possible. Use the excess icing that comes over the edge to cover the sides. If necessary add more icing to cover the sides of the cake with a smooth coat. If you have your cake on a cardboard round, do not let the icing extend over this board. If your cake is rounded, to smooth the icing, hold a 2 x 10-inch strip of cellophane at both ends and drag it over the cake, starting at the bottom. The cellophane will curve to the shape of the cake, unlike a metal spatula.

3. Chill the cake. Cakes crumbed in buttercream should be refrigerated for at least 15 minutes or until the buttercream has set. Cakes crumbed with Whipped Cream (see page 35) or Whipped Chocolate Ganache (see page 82) should be placed in the freezer just until set (30 minutes to 2 hours, depending on your freezer). (Do not remove cakes crumbed with Whipped Chocolate Ganache until just before glazing.)

ICING

For some of us it's all about the icing. Moms, dads, and children alike devour sweet and glorious icing with glee. Kids may be notorious for fighting over buttercream roses, but I've known some grown-ups who will polish off any icing other people leave on their plates. Whether it is my mom's rich and buttery Italian meringue buttercream (Kaye's Buttercream) or decadent Chocolate Glaze, you will find yourself enjoying icing more than ever, maybe even stealing a bite from a loved one, after trying our recipes.

Each type of icing lends itself to a different application. Buttercreams can be made textured or flat, whereas poured glazes have a smooth glow whether they ice a shaped or flat cake. See which style and flavor goes best with your dessert.

Old-Fashioned Icing on a Cake or Cupcake

Keep it simple. Envision the cake on the cover of a Betty Crocker box and you will know what I mean. Old-fashioned icings, like Kids' Buttercream and Matt's Fudge Icing, are a dream to work with. Not only are they easy to whip up, but their texture is fluffy and application to cakes is easy to master. A slight flourish of the spatula, and you are finished.

To achieve this look we recommend Kids' Buttercream, Peanut Butter Icing, Whipped Cream, or Matt's Fudge Icing (see pages 33–35).

1. To ice, simply place a nice-size dollop of frosting on top of your cupcake or little cake; for a standard cupcake we recommend 2 tablespoons of icing.

2. With a small metal spatula, spread the icing so that it covers all of the exposed cake. Then create a textured pattern on the cake by pushing into the icing with the spatula and then pulling straight up; or apply light pressure while moving the spatula randomly about the surface of the icing, then glide the spatula off at a 45-degree angle to end the pattern. Anyone can do this.

3. If you plan on adding sprinkles or chocolate shavings, do so right away because the old-fashioned icings tend to form a hard shell quickly.

Smooth (Flat) Icing on a Cupcake

Instead of going for the traditional icing on a cupcake, consider trying a more polished approach. The smooth icing makes a stylish backdrop for buttercream flowers or chocolate decorations.

To achieve this look we recommend Kaye's Buttercream or House Buttercream, although a less refined version can be done with Kids' Buttercream, Peanut Butter Icing, Whipped Cream, or Matt's Fudge Icing (see pages 33–35).

1. Place a nice-size dollop of icing on top of your cupcake; for a standard cupcake we recommend 2 tablespoons of icing.

2. With the full length of a small metal spatula, spread the icing up to, and slightly over, the edge of the cupcake; the blade of the spatula should face away from you as you push away and face toward you as you pull toward you. Keep the spatula level; do not be tempted to follow the curvature of the cupcake edge downward. The icing will be a little thicker on the edges as compared to the center.

3. Hold the blade of the spatula at a 30- to 45-degree angle to the edge of the cupcake, then, holding the cupcake at approximately eye level, with a downward motion of the spatula, scrape off the icing that runs over the edge of the cupcake. Rotate the cupcake and continue scraping off the excess icing. A nice beveled edge should form around the circumference of your cupcake.

4. If desired, roll this beveled edge in nonpareils or sprinkles.

Smooth (Flat) Icing on a Cake

It is very difficult to get icing smooth on a shaped cake, unless the sides and top are straight, as in our beach pail, or evenly curved like our shark; see below, Smooth (Flat) Icing on a Shaped Cake. Even with a standard round cake, mastering a smooth finish will take practice and patience, but the end results will be worth the effort.

To achieve this look we recommend Kaye's Buttercream or House Buttercream, although a less refined version can be done with Kids' Buttercream, Whipped Cream, Peanut Butter Icing, and Matt's Fudge Icing (see pages 33–35).

1. Prepare the icing for the final coat, coloring your buttercream as desired. Place the cake in the center of the turntable.

2. With a metal spatula, spread a small amount of icing evenly over the top of the cake.

3. Ice the sides of the cake. Load the spatula with icing and run the bottom edge of it along the contour of the cardboard or hover just above the crumb coat, being careful to keep the spatula upright. Hold the spatula perpendicular to and flush against the cardboard (or crumb coat) to ensure even distribution of the icing. Reload the spatula as needed until the sides are covered.

4. Smooth the sides by holding the spatula upright against the side of the cake. (Instead of a spatula we often use flat metal or stiff plastic scrapers to make our smooth finish. If you can get your hands on one, it makes the job of icing a lot easier.) Slowly spin the turntable without lifting the spatula from the cake's surface. Remove any excess icing with the spatula. This step is probably the most challenging to master. I find it helpful to have a container of hot water nearby to dip my spatula in before each pass across the cake (dry it off after each dip). The heat will melt the icing, giving it a smooth surface.

5. A lip of excess buttercream will have formed at the top edge of the cake. Use your spatula to gently sweep the excess buttercream toward the center around the entire circumference of the cake until the top is smooth and level.

6. Push the spatula under the cake (and cardboard) and use it as leverage to lift one side of the cake. Place your fingers under this area and drag the spatula to the opposite side of the cake. Carefully lift, with the spatula and fingers, and place the cake on its base. Remove your fingers first, then slide the spatula out; if there is a cardboard round under the cake use glue to adhere it to the base, otherwise a dab of icing will suffice.

Smooth (Flat) Icing on a Shaped Cake

- If your cake is rounded, to smooth the icing, hold a 2 x 10-inch strip of cellophane at both ends and drag the long edge of it over the cake, starting at the bottom. Continue around the circumference of the cake until it is smooth. The cellophane will curve to the shape of the cake, unlike a metal spatula.

- If your cake is square or has corners, first make sure there is enough icing on the top corners (level with the rest of the top). To smooth the sides, with a metal scraper or spatula flatten one side at a time. Work in one direction, using the excess icing that comes over the corner to help smooth the next side. For the last side, slice off the excess icing that comes over the corner. Use your spatula to gently sweep the lip of excess buttercream that forms on the top edge toward the center of the cake.

Simple Glaze on a Cake or Cupcake

To achieve this look we recommend using Simple Glaze (see page 36).

- While the cake or cupcake is still hot, with a rubber spatula or even a soup spoon, dollop the glaze on top (1 tablespoon for a cupcake or muffin and 2 to 3 tablespoons for a mini Bundt cake). Swish the spatula or spoon around until the glaze begins to run over the edge. Let the cake cool and the glaze will form a thin, hard crust as it sets.

- For a different look, drizzle the tops of cooled (un-iced) cakes. The glaze should not run and will hold a linear form. Just keep in mind that if you want the cake to stay fresher longer, it must be kept wrapped in an airtight container.

Chocolate Glaze on a Cupcake

Chocolate Glaze can raise the cupcake's standing to a sophisticated treat or allow the cupcake to bask in the glow of its own whimsy when encrusted with nonpareils or sprinkles. Prefreeze the cupcakes for at least an hour or overnight before glazing; this allows the glaze to chill faster, stay in place, and not drip off the cupcake's edge.

To achieve this look we recommend using Semisweet or Milk Chocolate Glaze or White Chocolate Glaze (see pages 34 and 36).

1. Prepare the glaze. Work with the chocolate glaze at body temperature (approximately 100°F). If you premade the glaze, gently reheat it in the top of a double boiler. Be careful not to over-heat the glaze or it will lose its shine, or crack when dry.

2. Take the cupcakes out of the freezer—just a few at a time so they do not stand long enough to sweat. Hold the cupcake firmly by the paper liner and invert it into the pot or bowl of melted glaze. Submerge the cupcake up to the paper line and move it about to ensure the entire surface is covered. Pull the cupcake straight up and gently spin it above the bowl by rotating your wrist, to allow any excess glaze to drip off. Flip the cupcake and carefully place it on a wire rack to set.

3. Allow the glaze to set for 3 to 5 minutes at room temperature before adding sprinkles or chocolate shavings.

Chocolate Glaze on a Cake

Unlike buttercream, which takes practice to get smooth, chocolate glaze pours over the pre-pared cake surface, hiding most imperfections. Because it is easy to work with, delicious, and beautiful, this is my favorite choice for icing a cake.

Freeze your cakes for one hour before glazing.

To achieve this look we recommend using Semisweet or Milk Chocolate Glaze or White Chocolate Glaze (see pages 34 and 36).

1. Work with the chocolate glaze at body temperature (approximately 100°F). If you premade the glaze, gently reheat it in the top of a double boiler. Be careful not to overheat the glaze or it will lose its shine, crack when dry, or cause the crumb coat to melt.

2. Place a wire cooling rack on a sheet pan and place the filled, crumbed, or plain cakes on top separated by 1 to 2 inches.

3. Pour the glaze into a liquid cup measure to make glazing easier, or pour or ladle the glaze directly around the top edge of the cake, allowing the glaze to run down the sides. Pour the remaining glaze on top. Immediately run a metal spatula over the top of the glaze to push the excess over the sides, being careful not to touch the cake itself. Make sure the sides are covered completely. Shake the sheet pan lightly to help the glaze settle. Let set for 3 to 5 minutes at room temperature before plating.

4. If you like, press chocolate shavings or chocolate sprinkles onto the sides of the cake.

5. Place the cake on its base; if there is a cardboard round under the cake use glue to adhere it to the base, otherwise a dab of glaze will suffice.

Piped Icing on a Cupcake or Cake

Instead of spreading icing on a cupcake or cake, place the icing into a pastry bag with a coupler and tip and pipe it on. A simple spiral of buttercream, piped out of a star tip, will suffice or you can be inventive and cover the top with small stars, dots, or flowers (see Flower Power, page 131). Basket weave, a traditional covering for cakes, takes a fun twist when it tops our Basket Cupcakes and our Straw Hat. Just keep in mind that if you want the cake to stay fresher longer, you must make sure the piping completely covers the cake surface, or consider crumbing your cake first (see page 24). See page 38 for more piping tips.

To achieve this look we recommend using Kaye's Buttercream or House Buttercream, although a less refined version can be done with Kids' Buttercream or Peanut Butter Icing (see pages 31–34).

pan ease

If you bake often at home this recipe is indispensable. Like most bakeries, we use pan ease to grease our pans. It is very economical and convenient, with a long shelf life. Just brush it on the pans and you are good to go.

In the bowl of an electric mixer, mix with a paddle attachment until smooth:

- 2 cups shortening
- ½ cup all-purpose flour

Using a whisk attachment add:

- ½ cup plus 1 tablespoon vegetable oil

At high speed, beat until light and fluffy.

Store at room temperature in an airtight container.

house buttercream ** YIELD: 4 ¾ CUPS

Unlike Kaye's Buttercream (see page 32), this icing contains some shortening. *Not only does this ingredient create a lighter flavor, it also gives this buttercream its pure whiteness, making it ideal for mixing with colors. We use high-ratio shortening, which can be found at any good cake decorating supply store, or online; high-ratio shortening does not affect the taste, but it does increase the buttercream's ability to accept color. If you can't find high-ratio shortening, substitute regular vegetable shortening.*

House Buttercream can be stored in an airtight container at room temperature for up to 3 days and in the refrigerator for up to 3 weeks. To use the chilled buttercream, bring it to room temperature and beat at medium speed in the bowl of an electric mixer until smooth and creamy. To speed up this process you can lightly reheat the buttercream, in its mixing bowl, over a hot-water bath, before beating.

In the bowl of an electric mixer at low speed, stir together:

- 3 cups confectioners' sugar
- ¼ teaspoon salt
- ½ teaspoon pure vanilla extract

With a whisk attachment, add and whip at low speed:

- ½ cup boiling water (⅓ cup on hot days)

Whip until smooth and cool.

Add and whip until smooth:

- 1½ cups high-ratio shortening
- 3 ounces (¾ stick) slightly chilled unsalted butter, cut into 1-inch pieces

Increase the mixer speed to medium-high. Whip until light, fluffy, and doubled in volume (10 to 20 minutes). If the buttercream still appears too soft, add butter 1 tablespoon at a time until it is a spreadable consistency.

There is no escaping the fact that this is buttercream at its purest. If you are among the naysayers that claim they don't like buttercream, hold off on your judgment until you try my mom's delicious buttercream atop your next cake.

Although this buttercream can be tinted, it is not ideal to use when you want to mix bright or rich colors, as the food coloring tends to bead up and does not combine fully with the buttercream. The high butter content also creates a subtle yellow tone to the buttercream which can mute some colors, making them less bright or pure.

Kaye's Buttercream can be stored in an airtight container at room temperature for up to 3 days and in the refrigerator for up to 3 weeks. To use the chilled buttercream, bring it to room temperature and beat at medium speed in the bowl of an electric mixer until smooth and creamy. To speed up this process you can lightly reheat the buttercream, in its mixing bowl, over a hot-water bath, before beating.

In a small saucepan, bring to a boil:

- ¼ cup water
- 1 cup plus 2 tablespoons sugar

Use a clean pastry brush and cold water to wash down any sugar crystals that form on the sides of the pan as the water heats. When the sugar comes to a boil, set a timer for 7 minutes, and let boil.

After 5 minutes, in the bowl of an electric mixer, begin to whip at high speed:

- ½ cup egg whites (about 6 large egg whites)

Whip until stiff. They should be done when the timer goes off.

With the mixer on high speed, slowly beat the sugar syrup into the egg whites, pouring the syrup to the side of the bowl to avoid the whip.

Continue to beat until the bowl is cool to the touch, about 10 minutes. Slowly add:

- ¾ pound (3 sticks) unsalted butter at room temperature, cut into 1-inch pieces

When the buttercream begins to jump out of the bowl, reduce the speed to low.

Mix in at low speed:

- 1 teaspoon pure vanilla extract

Beat until light and fluffy. At some points the mixture might look curdled. Just keep beating; it will become smooth again.

This is the kind of icing that grandmas across the country have been spreading on cakes for generations, probably because it is so easy to make: no eggs, no cooking, no worries. We call this ultrasweet frosting Kids' Buttercream, because most often it is found atop our cupcakes, which kids, and adults (secretly), devour. We also ice our Red Velvet cakes with this creamy concoction. Although this icing tints beautifully, we don't use it for delicate piping applications because it has a dense and slightly gritty texture that tends to break.

Kids' Buttercream can be stored in the refrigerator in an airtight container for 1 week. To use the chilled buttercream, bring it to room temperature and beat at medium speed in the bowl of an electric mixer until smooth and creamy. To speed up this process you can lightly reheat the buttercream, in its mixing bowl, over a hot-water bath, before beating.

Meringue powder can be found at baking supply stores and some supermarkets.

In the bowl of an electric mixer at medium-high speed, beat until creamy:

- 8 ounces (2 sticks) unsalted butter

Add all at once and beat at low speed until smooth:

- 4 cups (1-pound box) sifted confectioners' sugar
- 1 tablespoon meringue powder
- 1 teaspoon pure vanilla extract
- ¼ teaspoon salt

Add and beat until light and creamy:

- 2 tablespoons milk

FLAVORED BUTTERCREAM

chocolate buttercream: In a bowl, combine 2 to 3 ounces of melted, body temperature (100°F) semisweet chocolate per 1 cup of Kaye's Buttercream. Mix until smooth and completely blended, scraping down the sides of the bowl to prevent the chocolate from hardening and causing unmelted flecks in the buttercream.

praline buttercream: In a bowl, combine ⅓ cup of finely chopped praline (see page 167) per scant 1 cup of Kaye's Buttercream. Stir until combined.

coffee buttercream: In a bowl, dissolve 2½ teaspoons of instant espresso powder in 2½ teaspoons of hot water. Whisk in 1 cup of Kaye's Buttercream. Mix until smooth and completely blended.

dulce de leche buttercream: In a bowl, for every 1 cup of Kaye's Buttercream, mix in ¼ cup of Dulce de Leche (see page 101). Stir or whip until thoroughly combined and no lumps of dulce remain.

For all of you peanut butter lovers out there, here is a scrumptious twist on our Cream Cheese Frosting (from our first book, The Whimsical Bakehouse). *It is good enough to eat right off the spoon.*

Peanut Butter Icing can be stored in the refrigerator in an airtight container for 1 week. To use the chilled icing, bring it to room temperature and beat at medium speed in the bowl of an electric mixer until smooth and creamy. To speed up this process you can lightly reheat the icing, in its mixing bowl, over a hot-water bath, before beating.

In the bowl of an electric mixer at medium-high speed, beat until creamy:

- 2 ounces (½ stick) unsalted butter

Add and beat until creamy:

- 4½ ounces (one and a half 3-ounce packages) cream cheese
- ½ cup smooth peanut butter

Add all at once and beat at low speed until smooth:

- 1 cup sifted confectioners' sugar

Continue to beat at medium speed until light and fluffy.

For beginners and professionals alike this is the perfect icing. It covers cakes smoothly and beautifully and it is one of the richest, most refined, and most decadent chocolate icings *you can make. This glaze adds an elegant aura to any cake no matter how big or small, but you can also make it whimsical with the addition of sprinkles or chocolate decorations. This recipe can be made with semisweet or milk chocolate; the semisweet has a darker, richer glow. The icing can be used immediately or cooled and stored in the refrigerator in an airtight container for up to 2 weeks. Reheat slowly in a double boiler before using if chilled.*

In a double boiler or in a medium metal bowl placed over a hot-water bath, melt:

- 1½ pounds semisweet chocolate or milk chocolate, chopped into small pieces

In a small saucepan, heat over medium-high heat:

- 2 cups heavy cream
- 5 ounces (1 stick plus 2 tablespoons) unsalted butter

- ¼ cup light corn syrup

Stir until the butter melts, then continue to heat to just before the boiling point (bubbles will form around the pan's rim). Slowly pour the scalded liquid over the melted chocolate, whisking constantly until smooth. Strain the icing through a fine sieve.

matt's fudge icing*

What would life be like without fudge? My brother-in-law Doug certainly
would not find much pleasure in cake, brownies, or ice cream were it not for this creamy and sweet
chocolate classic. This recipe comes from my Uncle Matt (the other beloved baker in our family). This
fudge has iced his Triple-Layer Chocolate Cake at the Hudson House in Nyack, New York, for as long
as I can remember—a chocoholic's dream come true.

Matt's Fudge Icing can be stored in the refrigerator in an airtight container for 2 weeks. To use
the chilled icing, bring it to room temperature and beat at medium speed in the bowl of an electric
mixer until smooth and creamy. To speed up this process you can lightly reheat the icing in its mixing
bowl, over a hot-water bath, before beating.

In a small saucepan over low heat, mix together:

- ¼ cup sugar
- 2 large egg yolks
- ¾ cup heavy cream
- 1 teaspoon pure vanilla extract
- Pinch of salt

Whisk until the mixture is slightly thickened and coats the back of a wooden spoon (175–180°F on a candy thermometer).

Remove from the heat and whisk in until melted:

- 8 ounces finely chopped semisweet chocolate
- 3 ounces (¾ stick) unsalted butter, cut into pieces

Whisk in:

- ¼ cup light corn syrup
- 2 tablespoons sour cream

Transfer to a bowl, cover with plastic wrap, and chill for 1 hour to overnight.

whipped cream*

Ah, whipped cream. It's light enough that you don't feel too indulgent when it is
spread atop your cupcake, rich enough to give balance to your strawberry shortcake, and the perfect
accompaniment to practically anything sweet. For best results, we recommend preparing the whipped
cream right before serving or assembling your cakes. Any leftovers can be stored in an airtight con-
tainer in the refrigerator for up to 3 days. The whipped cream will break down as it sits in the refriger-
ator, so rewhip in the bowl of an electric mixer for 1 minute or until medium to stiff peaks form.

In the bowl of an electric mixer fitted with a whisk attachment, whip until stiff:

- 1½ cups heavy cream
- 2 tablespoons confectioners' sugar, sifted
- ½ teaspoon pure vanilla extract

white chocolate glaze*

White Chocolate Glaze can be tinted with food coloring to achieve a veritable rainbow of decorative effects. Little red ladybugs are brought to vibrant life with a coating of this glaze. For Halloween, tint the glaze orange and make a batch of jack-o'-lanterns. Without any food coloring, the icing is a rather elegant creamy yellow. The icing can be used immediately or cooled and stored in the refrigerator in an airtight container for up to 2 weeks. Reheat slowly in a double boiler before using if chilled.

In a double boiler or in a medium metal bowl placed over a hot-water bath, melt:

- 1½ pounds white chocolate (or white wafer chocolate), chopped into small pieces

In a small saucepan, heat over medium-high heat:

- 1 cup plus 2 tablespoons heavy cream
- 1 ounce (2 tablespoons) unsalted butter

Stir until the butter melts, then continue to heat to just before the boiling point (bubbles will form around the pan's rim). Slowly pour the scalded liquid over the melted chocolate, whisking constantly until smooth. Strain the icing through a fine sieve.

simple glaze*

When you are looking for an easy way to finish off a Bundt cake, pound cake, or even a cupcake, just whip up a batch of this glaze and you have yourself a dessert you'll proudly make your table's centerpiece. The icing is gooey and sweet, but let it sit and a thin, hard crust will form over the cake, sealing in moistness and adding an extra sweet kick to every bite.

We flavored the glaze with coffee, but there are myriad other flavors to choose from. Substitute lemon juice, orange juice, or milk, in the same proportions, for the hot coffee. This is really as simple as you can get.

Sift into a bowl:

- 1 cup confectioners' sugar, plus additional as needed

Slowly whisk in:

- 2 tablespoons hot coffee, plus additional as needed

If the icing is too thick, add more liquid; and if it is too thin, add more confectioners' sugar.

Use the glaze immediately or place plastic wrap directly on the surface of the glaze. It can be stored in the refrigerator for 1 week.

simple decorating tips

By adding hints of color or a simple chocolate decoration, you can turn a muffin into a cupcake or a plain Bundt cake into a birthday cake. The following list includes some quick and easy ideas for making a plain cake into a special cake without too much fuss.

- Sprinkles or nonpareils are the easiest way to add pizzazz to a little cake. All you need to get the little beads of color to adhere is a layer of icing (½ cup of nonpareils will cover up to 16 glazed cupcakes). You can even mix nonpareils or sprinkles into the Caramel Cake or Pound Cake, or replace the poppy seeds with nonpareils in the Lemon Poppy Cake before baking to create a colorful confetti cake.

- Drizzle dark chocolate or tinted white chocolate directly on the tops of your cooled cakes. This is a great and simple decoration for Bundt cakes. Release your inner Jackson Pollock and have a ball. To add an extra kick to your cake, drizzle the tops with chocolate and then, before the chocolate has hardened, add sprinkles or nonpareils.

- By baking your cake batter in shaped pans (such as hearts or stars) instead of just a cupcake or small cake pan, you can create a decorated treat without much effort. Just dust with confectioners' sugar or pour some delicious Chocolate Glaze (page 34) on top and call it a day.

- Use color! By simply tinting your icing, you are creating a decorated cake. Mix up a soft pastel buttercream or pump it up a few notches and go for screaming neon buttercream.

- If you don't want to be bothered making a more complex icing, try making our Simple Glaze (opposite page). It pours nicely over Bundt cakes and cupcakes to create a frosted treat.

- If you are making a design that calls for a small amount of buttercream and you don't feel like whipping up an entire batch just to use ¼ cup, you can buy a package of vanilla icing at the store. It won't taste as good, but it is a big time saver.

- If you are making cupcakes, find a paper cupcake liner that matches your theme.

- The presentation for your little cake can be just as much of a decoration as the cake itself. By choosing a fun serving dish, you can change your little cake into an eye-catching dessert. Add a moat of Raspberry Sauce (page 69) or Caramel Sauce (page 82) and your guests will be awed. When displaying many little cakes together, consider using a stack of pedestal cake plates or a wire pastry tree. Height has impact, especially when the star of the show is so small!

- To make a simple base for your baked creations, glue a doily to a cardboard round of the same size. Cardboard rounds can also be covered with decorative foil; double the cardboards for a stronger base.

piping tips

- Icing consistency, whether it is soft or hard, smooth or lumpy, affects the appearance of your piping applications. You can often firm up or soften the buttercream by chilling it in the refrigerator for a few minutes or by lightly melting it over a double boiler. To remove any lumps, whisk or stir the buttercream. Soft buttercream flows easily, making it ideal for lace or line work. Most other piping applications need icing of a medium consistency that is fluid yet holds its form. Flowers need a medium to firm icing to hold the petal's shape, but keep in mind that if the icing is too stiff it will break or crack while piping.

- Bag pressure is influenced by two factors: the twisting and the squeezing of the pastry bag. Use one hand to guide the bag while squeezing with the other, twisting the top of the bag occasionally to maintain pressure. By altering the pressure you squeeze with, you can control the flow of buttercream. Your goal is to apply consistent pressure while moving the tip or bag at a steady pace or rhythm. However, some piping applications, such as "popcorn," call for irregular bag pressure and irregular rhythm. At the end of a line or embellishment, stop applying pressure to the bag and quickly spiral the tip, pull the tip downward, or pull the tip to the side. These actions are referred to as tailing off, and they end piping applications with a clean stroke.

- Tip placement, unless otherwise noted, is usually at a 45-degree angle to the cake. Two common exceptions are dots and rosettes, for which the tip is perpendicular to the cake surface. To begin, touch the pastry tip to the surface of the cake where you want to start piping, allowing the icing to adhere to the surface. Lift up the tip as you begin to apply pressure. Do not drag the tip along the surface of the cake, as this will indent the surface; instead, lightly touch the surface of the cake or hover above it as you pipe.

chocolate

At the Bakehouse we use a wide variety of chocolates: unsweetened chocolate, semisweet chocolate, milk chocolate, white chocolate, baker's chocolate, confectioners' chocolate (also called wafer chocolate or candy coating), and cocoa powder, not to mention chocolate chips (regular, mini, and white). Each type is suited for different recipes and applications. With the exception of cocoa powder, there are a few tips that hold true for working with chocolate.

- Do not get any water in chocolate, as this will cause it to "seize." Seizing is when chocolate resolidifies and becomes lumpy. If you are working with confectioners' chocolate, to counteract any seizing that may occur on humid days, try whisking in a few drops of vegetable oil.

- Store chocolate in a cool, dry place—not in the refrigerator.

- It is best to work with chocolate in a room at room temperature (68°–70°F).

- Each type of chocolate has a slightly different melting point (between 104°F and 113°F, and 115°F for confectioners' chocolate), but when melted they should all be at a fluid state with a temperature ranging from 95° to 120°F. When chocolate is overheated it will become solid and unworkable. Semisweet, bittersweet, milk, white, and confectioners' chocolate can all easily be melted over a double boiler or in a microwave (see below). Chocolate chips, however, are not recommended for melting unless combined with other ingredients such as butter, because they get lumpy.

- Never melt chocolate directly over a heat source; always use indirect heat.

- For melting chocolate in the microwave: If not using wafers, coarsely chop the chocolate. Place it in a glass or microwave-safe bowl. For 1 to 2 cups of chocolate, microwave in 30-second intervals, stirring in between to ensure the chocolate does not burn. It will take approximately 1½ minutes to melt, but times will vary based on the room temperature, the amount of chocolate you are melting, and the power of your microwave. Stirring chocolate vigorously will often melt any remaining small pieces.

- For melting chocolate over a double boiler: Find a metal bowl that fits snuggly in a medium-size pot, or use a double boiler. Fill the pot one third full with water and bring to a light simmer (hot but not boiling). If not using wafers, coarsely chop the chocolate and place it in the bowl. Place the bowl onto the pot. Do not let the bottom of the bowl touch the water. Heat the chocolate, stirring often, until all of the chocolate has melted (approximately 15 minutes). Remove from the heat.

THE CHOCOLATE METHOD

In our first book, *The Whimsical Bakehouse: Fun-to-Make Cakes That Taste as Good as They Look,* I introduced the Chocolate Method. I often compare this decorative process to painting on glass because everything is done in reverse; details like highlights and shadows are applied first, followed by the background. Using a template as a guide, melted chocolate is piped or painted onto parchment paper. When the design is complete it is set aside to harden, and then it is carefully flipped to reveal the starfish, or ghost, or cheetah print.

The One-Color Chocolate Method, simply put, is much like a silhouette created out of chocolate or tinted white chocolate. The Multicolor Chocolate Method combines bold chocolate outlines and a multitude of colors to create cartoon-like designs. Taken a step farther, the Advanced Chocolate Method combines fine lines and painterly shadows and highlights to create realistic designs, from portraits to blooming flowers. Finally the Relief Chocolate Method takes elements of all of these techniques and adds dimension through over-piping or stacking segments.

Chocolate Method Tips

● At the Bakehouse we use wafer chocolate to make all of our playful "chocolate" designs. Wafer chocolate is also referred to as confectioners' chocolate or candy coating. Because wafer chocolate does not need to be tempered, it is easy to work with, so it is ideal for the novice or home cake decorator. Unfortunately if you are looking for the true taste of chocolate you will have to temper your own semisweet or milk chocolate because wafer chocolate is a bit of a misnomer. Although the dark wafer chocolate contains cocoa, it does not contain chocolate liquor or cocoa butter, both of which give real dark chocolate its depth and richness.

● Approximately 6 ounces of unmelted wafer chocolate is equivalent to approximately 1 cup unmelted wafer chocolate or ½ cup melted wafer chocolate. All the measurements listed in design directions are calibrated in unmelted cups but you can measure the wafer chocolate by the ounce or by the cup in the melted state.

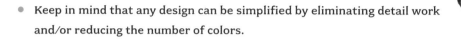

- When making designs, it is always a good idea to melt extra chocolate, and make extra designs, just in case a design breaks or you make a mistake and need more.

- Keep in mind that any design can be simplified by eliminating detail work and/or reducing the number of colors.

- If you are doing a multicolor design with outlines, make sure all of the colors overlap. This will prevent the design from breaking along the seams.

- The final design should be anywhere from $\frac{1}{8}$ to $\frac{1}{4}$ inch thick. The larger the design, the thicker it should be to ensure stability and ease of handling.

- Don't worry if you go outside the lines a little; the initial outline will maintain the definition of the design. In the worst-case scenario, you can carefully carve off the excess chocolate with a sharp paring knife, or score along a straight line and crack the excess off along the score.

- Consider drawing the design's outline with a color instead of just dark chocolate.

- To keep chocolates warm in the pastry cones, we use standard heating pads found at pharmacies. The temperature is hot but doesn't scald the chocolate as a double boiler or portable stove might do if the temperature isn't perfectly regulated. However, placing your chocolate bags on a sheet pan set over barely simmering water will do.

- Have all of your colors melted and placed in pastry cones before you begin. This will facilitate the decorating process.

- At the Bakehouse we often use cellophane instead of parchment paper to create our designs. Not only is it easier to see the template through the clear surface, but it leaves the chocolate nice and glossy.

- To remelt any chocolate on the paint brush, use a sheet pan over a pan filled with barely simmering water as a palette. Pushing the bristles about on this surface will remelt the chocolate. You have to work quickly, because when you are painting with thin layers, the chocolate dries quickly.

- A chocolate design can take anywhere from 5 minutes to 1 hour to set completely, depending on the room temperature and the size of the design. Because the chocolate designs in this book are for little cakes, the time range will usually be between 5 minutes and 15 minutes.

I will illustrate how to make an acorn using the Advanced/Relief Chocolate Method. The acorn is made in two segments (shell and nut) and then assembled after hardening, giving it added dimension. (See page 99 for Mini Acorn Cupcakes, which use these decorations.)

Use these directions as a guide for all of the Chocolate Method decorations in this book. You might have to change the palette, remove or add details, or adjust the amount of chocolate being melted, but in essence it is the same process. For a more in-depth look at the Chocolate Method, refer to our first book, *The Whimsical Bakehouse.*

WHAT YOU WILL NEED:
(MAKES APPROXIMATELY 10 ACORNS)

1 half-sheet pan

Parchment paper or cellophane

½ cup white wafer chocolate and
 ¼ cup dark wafer chocolate

Yellow and orange candy colors

Pastry cones

Small glass bowls

Rubber spatulas

Acorn template (page 170)

HOW TO

1. Photocopy or trace the acorn template. If you are making more than one acorn, you can trace one template and attach a long parchment tab, or handle, to it so that you can more easily move the template under the parchment paper to pipe out multiples without disrupting those you have already made. The other option is to trace or make as many photocopies of the template as you need. This may become problematic, however, when you need 40 of one design. Whichever way you choose, begin by placing the template onto a sheet pan or a flat surface. Cover the template with parchment paper or cellophane, and lightly secure with one or two pieces of tape.

2. Melt the white wafer and dark wafer chocolates separately. Set aside 1 tablespoon of white chocolate for the highlights. Tint the remaining white chocolate as follows: mix together approximately ¼ cup white chocolate with 2 drops of melted dark chocolate and one drop of yellow candy color to make the light brown. To make the dark brown, mix approximately ¼ cup white chocolate with 1 teaspoon melted dark chocolate and one drop of orange candy color. Pour the rest of the dark chocolate, white chocolate, and colored chocolates into 4

separate pastry cones. Keep the chocolates warm on a barely simmering double boiler or on a heating pad.

3. Cut a very small hole in the dark chocolate pastry cone. With a fine line, trace the outline of the acorn, including any interior crosshatching and details.

4. Pipe additional chocolate lines on the left edge of the shell and nut. Before these lines set, use a paintbrush to gently feather the chocolate toward the right and in a downward motion. You should still be able to see the parchment through these semitransparent shadows. Although the shadows overlap the line-work, they should not be applied so roughly as to wipe these initial lines off.

5. Cut a small hole in the white chocolate pastry cone and pipe a line along the right edge of the shell and a few thin lines following the contour of the nut. Before the lines on the shell set, use a paintbrush to gently feather the chocolate toward the left. Do not feather the nut lines.

6. Now cut medium holes in the colored bags. Fill in the nut with the tan and the shell with the brown. Set aside to harden.

7. When hardened, carefully flip the design and gently peel off the parchment paper.

8. Attach the shell to the nut with a dot of melted chocolate, gently holding them in place until the chocolate has set.

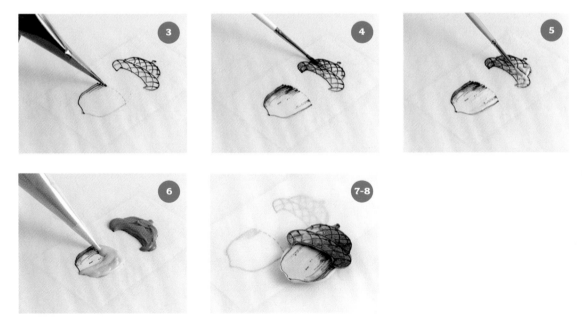

COLOR MIXING CHART

The buttercream colors below are mixed from a palette of red, neon brite pink, sunset orange, lemon yellow, neon brite green, leaf green, teal, royal blue, sky blue, violet, black, and buckeye brown liquid gel colors. The chocolate colors are mixed from a palette of red, pink, orange, yellow, green, royal blue, sky blue, violet, and black candy colors. Candy color is not available in brown; for those formulas, use melted dark wafer chocolate in place of brown coloring. You might not be able to mix a true sky blue or teal, depending on the range of colors available in the brand you buy; if these colors are important for your designs, I recommend buying a bag of pretinted wafer chocolate, or a jar of paste color for buttercream. When mixing colors, whatever colorant you are using, always err on the side of too little color as opposed to too much. Add color drop by drop. If a color is too dark, and you want to make it lighter, adding white buttercream or white chocolate doesn't always solve the problem. More often than not you end up adding cups of buttercream before reaching the desired color. Instead, start over and use the food coloring cautiously.

If you don't need a wide range of colors, you can just use blue, yellow, and red food coloring. These primary colors, in varying amounts and when mixed together in different proportions, can give you pinks, greens, oranges, purples, and more.

If you cannot find liquid gel colors, paste colors work just as well. Liquid colors can be used but the palette is limited and they are less concentrated. Use this chart as an approximate guide for mixing colors. Your results may vary depending on the brand and type of coloring you use. These formulas are based on drops of liquid gel colors per $1/4$ cup of House Buttercream and drops of candy colors per $1/4$ cup of melted white wafer chocolate.

color	buttercream with liquid gel colors	wafer chocolate with candy colors
RED	5 red	10 red
PALE PINK	scant drop neon pink or 1 red	scant drop pink or 1 red
PINK	2 neon pink	1 pink
NEON PINK	5 neon pink	3 pink
ORANGE	3 orange	4 orange
PALE ORANGE/PEACH	scant drop orange	1 orange

color	buttercream with liquid gel colors	wafer chocolate with candy colors
RUST	3 orange + 3 red	4 orange + 5 red
TERRA COTTA	5 orange + 1 brown + 1 red	8 orange + 8 drops dark chocolate
CORAL	1 orange + 2 neon pink	2 orange + 1 pink
DARK CORAL	2 orange + 4 neon pink	4 orange + 2 pink
YELLOW	2 yellow	4 yellow
SOFT BUTTERY YELLOW	scant drop yellow	scant drop yellow
STRAW YELLOW	2 yellow + scant drop orange + scant drop brown	5 yellow + 1 orange + 1 drop dark chocolate
GREEN	3 green + 1 brown	4 green + 12 drops dark hocolate
LIGHT GREEN	scant drop green + scant drop brown (optional)	1 green + 2 drops dark chocolate
NEON GREEN	2 green + 4 yellow or 3 neon brite green	3 green + 5 yellow
PALE NEON GREEN	1 green + 1 yellow or 1 neon brite green	1 green + 1 yellow
TEAL GREEN	4 teal or 1 green + 2 sky blue	2 sky blue + 1 green
LIGHT BLUE	1 royal or sky blue	1 royal or sky blue
SKY BLUE	3 sky blue	2 sky blue
ROYAL BLUE	5 royal blue	6 royal blue
PERIWINKLE	1 royal blue + 1 violet	1 royal blue + 1 violet
VIOLET / PURPLE	3 violet	3 violet
BRIGHT PURPLE	1 violet + 4 neon pink	1 violet + 2 pink
PALE VIOLET / LAVENDER	1 violet	scant drop violet or 1 pink + 4 chocolate
LIGHT BROWN	1 brown	15 drops dark chocolate + 1 orange (optional)
DARK BROWN	5 brown	45 drops dark chocolate + 2 orange (optional)
GRAY	1 black	1 black

ANYTIME LITTLE CAKES & MUFFINS

You don't need a special occasion to mix up a batch of these little cakes. For breakfast, as a treat with tea, or as a midnight snack, these recipes are perfect anytime.

Hidden within these pages is a little surprise for you: a collection of our best muffin recipes. We know; you are probably thinking: this is a cake book, why include muffins? Well, the way we see it, muffins may have become a breakfast staple, but even when occasionally packed with a bit more nutritional value, they are really just little cakes. Another added bonus: most muffin recipes are so easy to make you don't even need an electric mixer. Unless otherwise noted, all you need is a bowl and a wooden spoon.

Muffin batter can be made up to a week ahead and stored in an airtight container in the refrigerator. Just scoop and bake whenever you are craving a fresh and warm treat. Once baked, however, muffins are best eaten within the day. Wrap them in an airtight container and they will last a couple days longer, and if frozen they can last up to a month. When you are ready to eat your baked goodies, let them come to room temperature in their airtight container. To bring them back to full flavorful and textural life, just pop them in a 350°F oven for 5 minutes.

You will also find a variety of little cakes like Almond Coffee Cakes and Coffee Pecan Pound Cakes in this chapter. Like muffins, many of these cakes are traditionally associated with breakfast, but don't let that stop you from eating them whenever you like. We love Plum Kuchens for dessert and Blueberry Crumb Cakes as an after-school snack.

If you are looking for a wonderful way to save time when you are planning a party, consider making the anytime cakes in advance. They can be made and assembled in their pans, wrapped well in plastic wrap, and frozen (unbaked) for up to 2 weeks. Let the cakes thaw in the refrigerator overnight, then bring to room temperature (approximately 30 minutes) and bake as directed.

Some of the recipes in this chapter call for two or more pans to be used. This doesn't mean you have to run to the store. If you don't have enough pans to bake all of your little cakes at once, use just one pan and bake in batches. Since the baking times are so short, the batter can be left at room temperature.

corn muffins*

YIELD: 12 MUFFINS

Corn muffins are believed to be the first manifestation of a muffin ever made in America. Whoever baked the first one, thank you! That corn muffin evolved into countless other delicious muffins. This is our version of the classic. We love to slice them, spread them with butter, and then fry them on a griddle until they are golden brown and crispy. Scrumptious.

Grease the top of a 12-mold muffin pan and line it with paper liners. Preheat the oven to 350°F. Have all ingredients at room temperature.

In a large bowl, stir to blend:
- ¾ cup sugar
- ½ cup vegetable oil

Mix in:
- 2 large eggs

On a piece of wax paper, sift together:
- 1½ cups all-purpose flour
- 1 tablespoon baking powder
- ½ teaspoon salt

Transfer the dry ingredients to a medium bowl and add:
- 1½ cups cornmeal

Add the dry ingredients to the sugar and egg mixture alternately with:
- 1 cup milk

Mix just to combine.

Scoop the batter into the prepared molds, filling each to the top of the paper liner. Bake for 20 to 25 minutes, or until a cake tester inserted into the center of a muffin comes out clean. Cool on a wire rack for 5 to 10 minutes before removing the muffins from their pan.

blueberry muffins*

YIELD: 12 MUFFINS

Imagine waking up on a buzzing summer morning to the aroma of freshly baked blueberry muffins. That is better than any alarm clock! Add this light and sweet classic to your repertoire and make someone's morning unforgettable. You can use fresh or frozen blueberries, so you can enjoy these muffins year-round.

Grease and flour the top of a 12-mold muffin pan and line it with paper liners. Preheat the oven to 350°F. Have all ingredients at room temperature.

In the bowl of an electric mixer, beat at high speed until light and fluffy:
- 4 ounces (1 stick) unsalted butter
- 1⅓ cups sugar

Add and beat on medium speed to combine:
- 2 large eggs
- ¾ teaspoon pure vanilla extract

On a piece of wax paper, sift together:
- 2 cups all-purpose flour
- 2 teaspoons baking powder
- ½ teaspoon salt

Mix the dry ingredients into the butter and egg mixture at low speed just until combined.

Add and mix until combined:
- 1 cup buttermilk

Fold in:
- 9 ounces (2 cups) fresh or thawed frozen blueberries

Scoop the batter into the prepared molds, filling each to the top of the paper liner. Bake for 25 to 30 minutes, or until a cake tester inserted into the center of a muffin comes out clean. Cool on a wire rack for 5 to 10 minutes before removing the muffins from their pan.

zucchini muffins *

YIELD: 12 MUFFINS

Don't let the idea of using a vegetable in your morning treat turn you off,
because these muffins are delicious, moist, and sweet. At my mom's first bakery, the Runcible
Spoon, she had a customer we nicknamed "Zucchini Man" because, without fail, he would come in
every morning for his zucchini muffin. Perhaps you should make this muffin your morning ritual,
too. And if you are a chocoholic, believe it or not, these muffins are great with some chocolate
chips thrown into the batter.

Grease the top of a 12-mold muffin pan and line it with paper liners. Preheat the oven to 350°F. Have all ingredients at room temperature.

In a medium bowl, mix well:
- 2 cups sugar
- 1⅓ cups vegetable oil
- 4 large eggs
- 1 teaspoon pure vanilla extract

On a piece of wax paper, sift together:
- 3 cups all-purpose flour
- 1 teaspoon baking powder
- 1½ teaspoons baking soda
- 1 teaspoon salt
- 1 tablespoon ground cinnamon
- ¼ teaspoon ground cloves

Add the dry ingredients to the wet ingredients and mix to combine.

Add and mix just to combine:
- 1 cup chopped walnuts
- ¾ cup raisins
- 14 ounces (3 cups) grated zucchini (approximately 3 medium zucchini)

Scoop the batter into the prepared molds, filling each to the top of the paper liner. Bake for 20 to 25 minutes, or until a cake tester inserted into the center of a muffin comes out clean. Cool on a wire rack for 5 to 10 minutes before removing the muffins from their pan.

banana muffins *

My mom has to try the banana muffins at every bakery, deli, or restaurant she visits, and, in her "unbiased opinion," she says hers (the recipe below) are the best she has ever eaten. They are unbelievably moist and banana-y. The richness of the muffin may be attributed to the butter. Nuts are optional, but as any Hudson will tell you (Hudson is my mom's maiden name), nuts make anything better.

Grease the top of a 12-mold muffin pan and line it with paper liners. Preheat the oven to 350°F. Have all ingredients at room temperature.

In a medium bowl, mix well:
- 1 cup sugar
- 4 ounces (1 stick) unsalted butter, melted
- 2 large eggs

On a piece of wax paper, sift together:
- 2 cups all-purpose flour
- 1½ teaspoons baking soda
- ¾ teaspoon salt

Add the dry ingredients to the wet ingredients and mix to combine.

Add and mix just to combine:
- 1 cup mashed bananas (approximately 2 bananas)
- ½ cup chopped walnuts
- 2 tablespoons hot water

Scoop the batter into the prepared molds, filling each to the top of the paper liner. (Optional: Before baking, sprinkle ½ cup chopped walnuts over the tops of the muffins.) Bake for 20 to 25 minutes, or until a cake tester inserted into the center of a muffin comes out clean. Cool on a wire rack for 5 to 10 minutes before removing the muffins from their pan.

whole wheat blackberry muffins *

YIELD: 16 MUFFINS

This is my favorite muffin at the Bakehouse, partly because I can delude myself into thinking it is good for me (whole-wheat flour, blackberries). Bursts of blackberry tartness punctuate the subtle sweetness. How do you make a great muffin even better? Top it off with a sprinkling of buttery streusel.

Prepare one batch of Streusel Topping (page 59) and set aside. Any remaining streusel can be stored in a sealed container in the refrigerator.

Grease and flour the tops of three 6-mold muffin pans and line 16 of the molds with paper liners. Preheat the oven to 350°F. Have all ingredients at room temperature.

In a small bowl, whisk together just to combine:

- 6 ounces (1½ sticks) unsalted butter, melted
- 2 large eggs
- 2 cups buttermilk

In another medium bowl, stir together:

- 1¾ cups all-purpose flour
- 1¾ cups whole-wheat flour
- 1 cup sugar
- 2½ teaspoons baking powder
- 1½ teaspoons baking soda
- 1 teaspoon salt

Stir the egg and butter mixture into the dry ingredients, just until combined.

Add and stir just to combine:

- 2½ cups blackberries (fresh or frozen)

Scoop the batter into the prepared molds, filling each to the top of the paper liner. Sprinkle approximately 2 tablespoons of streusel over the top of each muffin. Bake for 20 to 25 minutes, or until a cake tester inserted into the center of a muffin comes out clean. Cool on a wire rack for 5 to 10 minutes before removing the muffins from their pans.

oatmeal muffins*

Instead of starting your day with a granola bar or a bowl of oatmeal,
we recommend baking a batch of these muffins. Filled with all of the goodness of oats, a sprinkling of golden raisins for sweetness, and buttermilk for that luscious bite, these tasty little numbers are sure to make you love breakfast again.

And if you are looking for a recipe that is not overly sweet, look no farther.

Grease the tops of three 6-mold muffin pans and line 16 of the molds with paper liners. Preheat the oven to 350°F. Have all ingredients at room temperature.

In a medium bowl, stir to blend:
- 1½ cups old-fashioned oats
- 1½ cups buttermilk
- ¾ cup golden raisins

Soak for one hour at room temperature.

Add and mix to combine:
- 6 ounces (1½ sticks) unsalted butter, melted
- 3 large eggs, lightly beaten
- 1½ cups light brown sugar, packed

On a piece of wax paper, sift together:
- 2¼ cups all-purpose flour
- 1 tablespoon baking powder
- 1¼ teaspoons baking soda
- 1½ teaspoons salt

Add the dry ingredients to the wet ingredients and mix to combine.

Scoop the batter into the prepared molds, filling each to the top of the paper liner. Bake for 25 to 30 minutes, or until a cake tester inserted into the center of a muffin comes out clean. Cool on a wire rack for 5 to 10 minutes before removing the muffins from their pans.

pumpkin muffins*

YIELD: 24 MUFFINS

Our customers ask for this delicious muffin year-round, but when the leaves start to fall in October we really begin to crave it. It is subtly spicy with an overtone of pumpkin warmth, just perfect for a crisp autumn morning. Save the top for last since it is encrusted with our delicious butter streusel.

Prepare one recipe of Streusel Topping (page 59). Set aside.

Grease the tops of two 12-mold muffin pans and line them with paper liners. Preheat the oven to 350°F. Have all ingredients at room temperature.

In a large bowl, mix to combine:
- 3 cups sugar
- ¾ cup plus 2 tablespoons vegetable oil
- 3 extra-large eggs
- 1 15-ounce can of plain pumpkin purée

On a piece of wax paper, sift together:
- 3¼ cups all-purpose flour
- 2½ teaspoons baking soda
- 2 teaspoons salt
- 2 tablespoons plus 1 teaspoon ground cinnamon
- 2 teaspoons ground nutmeg
- 1 teaspoon ground cloves
- Pinch of allspice

Add the dry ingredients to the wet ingredients and mix to combine.

Add and stir just to combine:
- 1 cup chopped walnuts
- ¾ cup golden raisins

Scoop the batter into the prepared molds, filling each to the top of the paper liner. Sprinkle approximately 2 tablespoons of streusel over the top of each muffin. Bake for 25 to 30 min-utes, or until a cake tester inserted into the center of a muffin comes out clean. Cool on a wire rack for 5 to 10 minutes before removing the muffins from their pans.

coffee chocolate chip muffins*

YIELD: 18 MUFFINS

You won't believe you are eating a muffin when you bite into these flavorful gems packed with rich coffee flavor and overflowing with chocolate chips. Our recipe comes from one of our favorite former employees, Monica Lender. It was her favorite and it is beloved by family and customers alike. My mom still brings two of these home every weekend to enjoy on the days she is being "bad," and sometimes she brings three, including one for my husband, Luiz.

Grease the tops of three 6-mold muffin pans and line them with paper liners. Preheat the oven to 350°F. Have all ingredients at room temperature.

In the bowl of an electric mixer, beat at high speed until light and fluffy:

- 12 ounces (3 sticks) unsalted butter
- 1 cup granulated sugar
- ½ cup light brown sugar, packed
- 2 large eggs
- 5 tablespoons instant espresso powder

On a piece of wax paper, sift together:

- 4 cups all-purpose flour
- 2 tablespoons baking powder
- ¼ teaspoon salt

At low speed, add the dry ingredients to the butter mixture and mix until just combined.

Still at low speed, add and mix until just combined:

- 1 cup milk
- 6 ounces (1 cup) chocolate chips

Scoop the batter into the prepared molds, filling each to the top of the paper liner. Bake for 20 to 25 minutes, or until a cake tester inserted into the center of a muffin comes out clean. Cool on a wire rack for 5 to 10 minutes before removing the muffins from the pans.

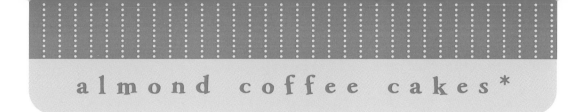

almond coffee cakes*

During the writing of our first book, we wooed our publisher with sweet treats. One of the cakes we took them was our Almond Coffee Cake, and it was a hit. After much begging for the recipe, finally, here it is. Enjoy.

CRUMBED ALMONDS

Pulse in a food processor until finely chopped:

- ⅓ cup granulated sugar
- 1 cup almonds
- 1½ teaspoons ground cinnamon

Set aside.

BATTER

Grease and flour 10 molds of a 12-mold mini square pan. Preheat the oven to 350°F. Have all ingredients at room temperature.

In the bowl of an electric mixer, beat at high speed until light and fluffy:

- 4 ounces (1 stick) unsalted butter
- ½ cup granulated sugar
- ½ cup light brown sugar, packed

Continue beating at medium speed and add:

- 1 large egg

Add and beat on medium speed to combine:

- 1 cup sour cream
- 1 teaspoon pure vanilla extract

In a small bowl, stir together:

- 1 cup all-purpose flour
- 1½ teaspoons baking powder
- Pinch of salt

Mix the dry ingredients into the butter and egg mixture at low speed just until combined.

Scoop 2 generous tablespoons of batter into each prepared mold. Spread 1 tablespoon of the crumbed almonds on top, followed by 2 generous tablespoons of batter. Finish with a sprinkling of crumbed almonds. Bake for 25 to 30 minutes, or until a cake tester inserted into the center of a cake comes out clean. Cool on a wire rack for 10 to 20 minutes before turning the cakes out of their pans. Once turned over, invert immediately to keep the crumbed almonds on top.

blueberry crumb cakes*

YIELD: 12 CRUMB CAKES

Our crumb cakes practically melt in your mouth. Unlike some crumb cakes that use a shortening-based crumb topping that can be sandy or dry, our crumb topping is made with—you guessed it—butter, so it is moist to the last bite. We add blueberries in the summer and apples in the fall. Try your favorite seasonal fruit.

We found the crumb-cake paper liners online (www.kingarthurflour.com). If you can't find them, grease and flour a jumbo muffin pan.

STREUSEL TOPPING

In the bowl of an electric mixer, using a paddle attachment, mix:

- 1 cup all-purpose flour
- ¼ cup light brown sugar, packed
- ⅓ cup granulated sugar
- 4 ounces (1 stick) cold unsalted butter, cut into ½-inch cubes
- 2 teaspoons ground cinnamon
- Pinch of salt

Continue mixing until pea-size bits of streusel form.

Set aside.

BATTER

Place twelve 3 x 1-inch crumb cake paper liners on a cookie sheet or half-sheet pan. Preheat the oven to 350°F. Have all ingredients at room temperature.

In the bowl of an electric mixer, beat at high speed until light and fluffy:

- 5 ounces (1 stick plus 2 tablespoons) unsalted butter
- 1½ cups granulated sugar
- ½ teaspoon pure vanilla extract

Add and beat on medium speed to combine:

- 2 large eggs

On a piece of wax paper, sift together:

- 2 cups all-purpose flour
- 2 teaspoons baking powder
- 1 teaspoon salt

Mix the dry ingredients into the butter and egg mixture at low speed just until combined.

Add and mix until combined:

- ¾ cup milk

Fold in:

- 2 cups (1 pint) fresh or thawed frozen blueberries

Divide the batter evenly among the paper liners. Spread ¼ cup of streusel on top of each. Bake for 22 to 28 minutes, or until a cake tester inserted into the center of a cake comes out clean. Cool on a wire rack for 5 to 10 minutes.

coffee pecan pound cakes*

Initially our Coffee Pound Cake was paired with the usual suspect: chocolate chips. But while experimenting with other add-ins we sampled one cake baked with pecans. We liked the way the pecans' sweet warmth brought out, instead of overwhelmed, the robust coffee flavor. Of course, you can still throw a handful of chocolate chips in for good measure.

We also smothered the little Bundts with a coffee-flavored Simple Glaze. It adds an attractive shine and a delicious jolt of flavor.

Grease and flour 10 molds of two 6-mold mini Bundt pans. Preheat the oven to 350°F. Have all ingredients at room temperature.

In the bowl of an electric mixer, beat at high speed until light and fluffy:
- 10 ounces (2½ sticks) unsalted butter

Add and beat well at high speed:
- 6 ounces (2 3-ounce packages) cream cheese
- 2 tablespoons instant espresso powder

Add and cream at high speed until light and fluffy:
- 1½ cups sugar

Add and mix well at medium speed:
- 2 tablespoons sour cream
- 1 teaspoon pure vanilla extract

Add one at a time, mixing well after each addition:
- 4 large eggs

On a piece of wax paper, sift together:
- 2¼ cups cake flour
- 2 teaspoons baking powder
- ¼ teaspoon salt

Add the dry ingredients to the butter and egg mixture and mix on low speed until smooth.

Stir in by hand:
- 1 cup chopped toasted pecans (see Note)

Place the batter into a pastry bag. Pipe it so that each prepared mold is three-quarters full. If you don't have a pastry bag, carefully spoon the batter into the molds. Bake for 20 to 25 minutes, or until a cake tester inserted into the center of a cake comes out clean. While the cakes are baking, prepare a Simple Glaze (page 36) and set aside. Cool the cakes on a wire rack for 15 to 20 minutes before turning them out of their pans. While the cakes are still warm to hot, spread the Simple Glaze on top (see page 28).

NOTE:

To toast pecans, place the nuts on an ungreased sheet pan. Bake at 350°F for 12 to 15 minutes or until fragrant. Let cool.

plum kuchens*

YIELD: 14 KUCHENS

Our testers, coworkers, and family agree, hands down, this is the best recipe.
Envision a late summer brunch replete with a squash and onion frittata, sweet potato home fries,
and these delicious plum mini kuchens. But the nutty streusel, plum, and cake aren't just perfect for
brunch; they also make a wonderful light dessert or sweet bite to go with your coffee.

At the Bakehouse we make kuchens (Kuchen is German for "cake") year-round. We replace plums
with other seasonal fruits such as apples, pears, peaches, or mangos.

TOPPING

Pulse in a food processor until finely chopped:
- 1½ tablespoons all-purpose flour
- ¾ cup light brown sugar, packed
- 1½ cups pecans
- 1½ teaspoons ground cinnamon

Add and process until pea-size bits of dough form:
- 3 ounces (¾ stick) cold unsalted butter, cut into ½-inch cubes

Set aside.

BATTER

Grease the tops of three jumbo muffin pans and line 14 molds with large foil or paper liners. Preheat the oven to 350°F. Have all ingredients at room temperature.

In a small bowl, combine:
- 1½ pounds pitted and finely cubed plums
- 2 tablespoons granulated sugar
- 1 teaspoon ground cinnamon

Set aside.

In the bowl of an electric mixer, beat at high speed until light and fluffy:
- 8 ounces (2 sticks) unsalted butter
- 1 cup granulated sugar
- ¾ cup light brown sugar, packed

Add and beat on medium speed to combine:
- ¾ cup sour cream

Continue beating at medium speed and add, one at a time:
- 3 large eggs

At low speed, add and mix just to combine:
- ¾ teaspoon pure vanilla extract
- 1 teaspoon fresh lemon juice

The batter may look curdled.

In a medium bowl, stir together:
- 2¾ cups all-purpose flour
- 1½ teaspoons baking powder
- 1½ teaspoons baking soda
- 1 teaspoon salt

Mix the dry ingredients into the butter and egg mixture at low speed just until combined.

Fold in the plum mixture.

Fill each lined mold three-quarters full. Divide the topping evenly over the kuchens. Bake for 25 to 30 minutes, or until a cake tester inserted into the center of a cake comes out clean. Cool on a wire rack for 10 to 20 minutes before turning the kuchens out of their pans. Once turned over, invert to keep the nut topping on top.

SPECIAL OCCASION LITTLE CAKES

Now it is time to combine my mom's wonderful recipes with some of my fun decorations.

Whether it is Carrot Cake baskets for Easter, classic vanilla Make a Wish Cupcakes for—you guessed it—your birthday, or Big Bang Pistachio Truffles when you just can't survive another night without chocolate, this chapter has a little cake for almost every special occasion.

All you really need to start the decorating process is a fun baking pan. Take the Rose Is a Rose cakes. The individual molds are shaped like small roses, so you don't need to do anything to these lovely delights; just bake and serve. While the Nostalgic Nibbles are decorated simply with a dusting of confectioners' sugar, other little cakes, such as the 3-D beach pail, are complex. But, if you are up for the challenge of creating a mini masterpiece, you will be rewarded with oohs and aahs from your family and friends. Keep in mind that these more difficult designs can be simplified by reducing the number of colors, or by making fewer and simpler chocolate decorations.

When my mom and I plan events, we try to match the flavors of the cake with the design or the season. Although it can be enjoyed year-round, apple cake is an edible representation of autumn. Pineapple upside-down cake combines a tangy and tropical sweetness with a rich, buttery cake, making it perfect after a summer barbecue or as a midwinter reminder that somewhere the sun is shining brightly. And chocolate ganache, cookie crumbs, and Chocolate Butter Cake bring the Flower Pots to life, hinting at the rich dark soil beneath the buttercream violets.

To create a visual delight, display your little cakes on interesting plates or pastry trees. The Raspberry Cheesecakes are plated with a tart and sassy raspberry sauce. Not only is the sauce a delicious accompaniment, but the red color beautifully accents the single berry nestled in the cheesecake. Our Flower Power cupcakes become a gorgeous bouquet when they are arranged on stacked cake pedestals, ideal for a wedding reception or a party centerpiece.

strawberry shortcakes *

You can make a fresh fruit filling for just about any cake, but nothing comes close to the real deal: shortcake. This slightly sweet biscuit is cut in half and filled with fresh strawberries, blueberries, and a generous dollop of whipped cream. Instead of a berry medley, take advantage of the delicious August peach crop, or for an exotic twist try mangos with fresh ginger (see Variation).

We cut out our shortcakes with a star cookie cutter, and they always dazzle on the Fourth of July. Experiment with other simple cookie cutters, such as hearts for Valentine's Day or flowers for a garden party.

SHORTCAKE

Preheat the oven to 350°F. Line a cookie sheet or half-sheet pan with parchment paper.

Pulse in a food processor just to combine:
- 2½ cups all-purpose flour
- 4 teaspoons baking powder
- ½ teaspoon salt
- ¼ cup brown sugar, firmly packed

Add and pulse until pea-size bits of dough form:
- 5 ounces (1¼ sticks) cold unsalted butter

Transfer the butter-flour mixture to a medium bowl. Add and mix until just combined:
- ¾ cup cold milk

If the batter appears too dry, add cold milk 1 tablespoon at a time until the dough just comes together.

Transfer the dough from the bowl to a lightly floured work surface, knead briefly, and then roll out to ½ to ¾ inch thick. Cut out the dough using a 4-inch star cookie cutter. Place the 8 stars 2 inches apart on the prepared pan. Lightly brush the tops of the stars with milk (you will need approximately 2 tablespoons), then sprinkle with granulated sugar.

Bake for 20 to 25 minutes or until golden. Place the pan on a wire rack to cool completely.

FRUIT FILLING

In a bowl combine:
- 2 pints sliced strawberries
- 1 pint blueberries
- 2 tablespoons granulated sugar

Set aside at room temperature for 30 minutes to 2 hours, to let the juices form.

VARIATION

Mango filling: Follow the directions above for fruit filling, replacing the strawberries and blueberries with 2 chopped mangos. To add a bit more zing, add the juice of half a lime and finely grated fresh ginger to taste.

SHORTCAKE ASSEMBLY

Prepare one recipe of Whipped Cream (page 35).

With a serrated knife slice the stars in half horizontally. Place the shortcake bottoms on their serving plates. Scoop approximately ½ cup of fruit on top of each bottom. Dollop whipped cream on top of the fruit. Gently replace the shortcake top. Do not press down. Serve immediately.

raspberry cheesecakes**

YIELD: 15 CHEESECAKES

As July rolls around and the raspberries are ripe for the picking, make a batch of these tiny delights to celebrate the summer's bounty, or spread the love on Valentine's Day by boxing up a heart-shaped cheesecake for everyone important in your life.

The raspberry sauce is delicious plated beneath these cheesecakes or on a scoop of vanilla ice cream.

RASPBERRY SAUCE (YIELD: ⅔ TO ¾ CUP)

In a food processor, combine and mix until puréed:

- 1 six-ounce container fresh raspberries, gently washed and picked over
- 1 to 2 tablespoons sugar
- 1 tablespoon fresh lemon juice or Framboise liqueur

Strain into a bowl to remove the seeds. Set aside.

Store in the refrigerator in an airtight container.

GRAHAM CRACKER CRUST

Grease 15 molds of two 12-mold mini heart cheesecake pans and wrap the bottom of the pans with aluminum foil.

In a small bowl, mix:

- ¾ cup finely crushed graham crackers
- 1 tablespoon sugar

Stir in:

- 2 tablespoons plus 1 teaspoon melted unsalted butter

Divide the crumb crust evenly among the prepared molds (about 1 tablespoon per mold). Press firmly onto the bottom.

FILLING

Preheat the oven to 350°F. Have all ingredients at room temperature.

In the bowl of an electric mixer, beat at medium speed until smooth:

- 12 ounces (one and a half 8-ounce packages) cream cheese

Scrape the bowl down often while beating.

Gradually beat in:

- ½ cup sugar
- 1 tablespoon all-purpose flour

When the sugar and flour are combined and the batter is smooth, scrape the bowl again. Add and mix at low speed until combined:

- 2 teaspoons grated lemon zest
- 2 tablespoons fresh lemon juice

Add and mix just until smooth:

- 2 large eggs

Pour the filling into the crust.

Insert into the center of each cheesecake:

- 1 large raspberry (15 raspberries in total)

Place the pans in a larger pan and fill the larger pan with ½ inch of hot water. Bake for 18 to 22 minutes or until set. Let the cheese-cakes sit at room temperature for 20 minutes before unmolding. To remove the cheesecakes from the pan, push a wooden spoon through the pan opening under each cheesecake. With a metal spatula remove the metal bottom from each cheesecake. Serve the cheesecakes warm or at room temperature. Alternatively, store the cheesecakes in the refrigerator in an airtight container for up to 2 days. Remove the cheesecakes from the refrigerator 2 hours before serving. Plate with the raspberry sauce.

falling leaves *

Thanksgiving at the Bakehouse is wildly busy, but I always take time to roam the streets looking for saplings with green leaves that have not yet fallen to the ground in a flurry of yellow and orange. It is like a treasure hunt. When I do find the perfect tree, I pluck the leaves off and scurry back to the bakery. These maple and oak leaves are given a gentle bath, patted dry, and then painted with chocolate. This is a classic technique among decorators and chocolatiers, who often use rose leaves. Instead of using dark chocolate, I pay homage to autumn's vibrant colors and paint my leaves yellow, orange, and rust. Because leaves have a thin layer of wax, chocolate doesn't stick to them. So when the leaf is peeled away you are left with a strikingly realistic chocolate leaf, embossed with all of the veins and intricacies of the real leaf.

Cake
12 Pumpkin Spice Cheesecakes (page 72)

Decoration
1 cup white wafer chocolate to make 12 leaves

Colors
yellow, red, and orange candy color

Miscellaneous
1 mini cheesecake pan, a small sable or acrylic paint brush, 1 half-sheet pan, parchment paper, 12 freshly picked small green leaves

HOW TO

1. Pick 12 leaves from nonpoisonous trees; we used small maple and oak leaves, taking care to leave some of the stem intact. Rose leaves work well if you do not have access to the deciduous trees. Gently clean the leaves in mild soapy water. Rinse well and place the leaves between paper towels. Pat dry.

2. Melt the white wafer chocolate (see page 39). Divide the chocolate evenly among three small bowls. Using the Color Mixing Chart on pages 44—45, tint one bowl rust, one orange, and one yellow.

3. Hold a leaf by the stem and gently rest the leaf over your cupped fingers or palm. With a paintbrush, paint the chocolate on the top of the leaf, dragging the chocolate up to the edge but not over it. The leaf can be one color or multicolored (lightly swirl the colors together). The chocolate should be at least ⅛ inch thick. Set the leaf on a parchment-lined sheet pan to harden. To make the leaf look like it is fluttering in the wind, drape part of the leaf over a wooden spoon and let it harden.

4. When hardened, carefully peel the leaf off the chocolate. If you let the chocolate set overnight the leaves are easier to remove.

5. Place one leaf on top of or adjacent to each cheesecake.

pumpkin spice cheesecakes**

YIELD: 12 MINI CHEESECAKES

When I was in college, my mom would send me care packages filled with chocolate chip cookies for my friends and gingersnap cookies all for me. So I was hooked when she told me these autumn cheesecakes combine the snap of our ginger cookie crust with the warmth of pumpkin and fall spices. You might find yourself saying bye-bye to pumpkin pie and hello to pumpkin cheesecake at your next Thanksgiving dinner.

GINGERSNAP CRUST

This recipe makes a lot of cookies, so we recommend baking only what is needed for this recipe. On a lightly floured board roll any leftover dough into logs. Wrap the logs in plastic wrap and freeze for up to 2 months. Remove the logs from the freezer and slice and bake whenever you want gingersnaps.

Line a cookie sheet or half-sheet pan with parchment paper. Grease one 12-mold mini cheesecake pan (the molds should be 2 inches in diameter; see the Cake Pan Chart on pages 16—17). Wrap the bottom of the cheesecake pan with aluminum foil. Preheat the oven to 350°F. Have all ingredients at room temperature.

In the bowl of an electric mixer at medium speed, cream until fluffy:
- 8 ounces (2 sticks) unsalted butter
- 1¼ cups sugar

Add and mix until smooth:
- 1 large egg
- ¼ cup molasses
- 1½ teaspoons vinegar

On a piece of wax paper, sift together:
- 2½ cups all-purpose flour
- 1 teaspoon baking soda
- 1 tablespoon plus 1 teaspoon ground ginger
- ½ teaspoon ground cinnamon
- ¼ teaspoon ground cloves
- Pinch of salt

Add to the butter mixture and mix at low speed until well combined.

Chill the dough, while it is still in the mixing bowl, for 10 minutes. Shape a portion of the dough into 12 ¾-inch balls. (Freeze the remaining dough; see headnote.) Arrange the balls 2 inches apart on the prepared cookie sheet. Bake the cookies for 8 to 10 minutes or until lightly colored. Let the cookies cool on the pan for 5 minutes, then, using a 2-inch round cookie cutter, cut out circles from the center of each cookie. Save the leftover edges for a snack. Place one cookie round in the bottom of each prepared cheesecake cup.

PUMPKIN FILLING

Preheat the oven to 350°F. Have all ingredients at room temperature.

In the bowl of an electric mixer, beat at medium speed until smooth:
- 12 ounces (one and a half 8-ounce packages) cream cheese

Scrape down the bowl often while beating.

Gradually beat in at medium speed:
- ⅓ cup brown sugar, packed
- 2 tablespoons all-purpose flour
- 2 tablespoons heavy cream

Add and stir to combine:
- ¼ cup canned pumpkin purée
- ½ teaspoon ground cinnamon
- ¼ teaspoon ground ginger
- ⅛ teaspoon allspice
- ⅛ teaspoon ground nutmeg
- 2 tablespoons finely chopped crystallized ginger (optional)

Add one at a time at low speed:
- 2 large eggs

Beat only until the eggs are fully incorporated. Pour the filling over the gingersnap crust in the prepared molds.

Place the pan in a larger pan and fill the larger pan with ½ inch of hot water. Bake for 20 to 25 minutes or until set. Let the cheesecakes sit at room temperature for 20 minutes before unmolding. To remove the cheesecakes from the pan, push a wooden spoon through the pan opening under each cheesecake. With a metal spatula remove the metal bottom from each cheesecake. Serve the cheesecakes warm or at room temperature. Alternatively, store the cheesecakes in the refrigerator in an airtight container for up to 1 week. Remove the cheesecakes from the refrigerator 2 hours before serving.

matt's upside-down cakes*

YIELD: 12 CAKES

My mom isn't the only amazing baker in her family. My uncle Matt Hudson is also known for his amazing dessert creations. Every time I go to his restaurant, the Hudson House in Nyack, New York, I can't resist getting one of his upside-down cakes. They change seasonally from pear to plum. When we found these mini upside-down baking molds at Williams-Sonoma, we knew we had to try pineapple. We thank Matt for his recipe, and I think you'll be thanking him, too, once you mix up a batch.

Lightly butter two 6-mold mini pineapple upside-down pans, or two 6-mold cupcake pans if making pear or plum upside-down cakes (see Note). Preheat the oven to 350°F. Have all ingredients at room temperature.

In a saucepan, melt:
- 3 ounces (¾ stick) unsalted butter

Add and whisk until combined:
- 1 cup firmly packed light brown sugar

Pour 1½ tablespoons of the butter-sugar mixture into each mold.

In the center of each mold place one slice of peeled and cored fresh or canned pineapple and one candied or canned cherry (12 pineapple slices and 12 cherries in total), or one slice of plum or pear (12 slices in total).

In the bowl of an electric mixer, combine:
- 2¼ cups all-purpose flour
- 2¼ cups granulated sugar
- 1 tablespoon cardamom
- 1¾ teaspoons baking soda
- ¾ teaspoon salt

Add and mix to combine:
- ¾ cup vegetable oil
- 3 large eggs

Mix in:
- ¾ cup (6 slices) coarsely grated pineapple with accumulated juice
- 1 tablespoon grated peeled fresh ginger

Divide the batter among the prepared pans.

Bake for 20 to 25 minutes or until a cake tester inserted into the center of a cake comes out clean. The tops should spring back when lightly pressed. Let the pan cool on a wire rack for no longer than 5 minutes, then place a sheet pan or large plate on top of the upside-down pan and invert. The pineapple cakes should unmold easily. They are best served warm, or refrigerate in an airtight container for up to 2 days, and reheat for 10 minutes at 350°F.

NOTE:

Substitute ¾ cup grated pear or plum (approximately 1 to 2 pears or 3 to 4 plums) for the grated pineapple when making pear or plum upside-down cakes.

nostalgic nibbles and devilish delights*

Here are some snacks that will have you skipping down memory lane.
Our renditions of the classic Twinkie and Devil Dog are even better than the originals since they are home-baked and fresh. Kids will adore them, and they will make you feel like a kid again.

We fill these treats with light whipped cream or Dulce de Leche—whatever strikes your fancy. Milk Chocolate Glaze is optional, but it adds another dimension of flavor. Serve with a cup of chilled milk and you are set.

Cake
16 Caramel Cake Twinkies minus the chips (page 79), or 18 Devil's Food Cake Twinkies (page 78), cooled

Filling
Whipped Cream (page 35) or 1½ cups Dulce de Leche (page 101)

Icing
¼ cup confectioners' sugar or 1 recipe Milk Chocolate Glaze (see page 34)

Tip
12 round tip or comparable

Miscellaneous
pastry bag, coupler, sifter for confectioners' sugar, or wire rack and half-sheet pan if glazing (optional 2 tablespoons melted chocolate for decorative drizzling)

HOW TO

1. Prepare the Dulce de Leche, if needed.

2. Bake the cakes and let them cool completely.

3. Prepare the Milk Chocolate Glaze, if needed. Prepare the Whipped Cream, if needed.

4. Place the Whipped Cream or Dulce de Leche into a pastry bag with a coupler and a #12 round tip. Insert the tip of the pastry bag into the center bottom of the cake and squeeze. Continue squeezing until the cake begins to swell in your hands or until the filling just begins to seep out around the tip's edge. Insert the tip again to the left and right of the center, being sure to stay at least ½ inch from the ends.

5. If you are keeping it simple, place the confectioners' sugar in a sifter and dust the tops of the filled cakes.

6. If glazing, freeze the filled cakes for 30 minutes. Once chilled, arrange the cakes 1 inch apart on the wire rack placed over the sheet pan. Ladle or pour the glaze over the tops. Remove the cakes from the rack with a metal spatula and plate.

7. Drizzle the tops with melted chocolate for added effect, if using.

8. For fullest flavor, serve the cakes at room temperature.

devil's food cake*

YIELD: 18 CUPCAKES OR 18 DEVILISH DELIGHTS

This versatile Devil's Food Cake is great baked in cupcake liners, Twinkie pans, or standard round cake pans. Smother it in Matt's Fudge Icing (page 35) or make it more angelic with a coating of Whipped Cream (page 35). Some recipes call for additional red dye; instead, the extra baking soda gives this recipe a red tint.

If you are making Devilish Delights (page 76), grease 18 molds of three Twinkie pans. If you are making cupcakes, grease the tops of three 6-mold muffin pans and line them with paper liners. Preheat the oven to 350°F. Have all ingredients at room temperature.

In the bowl of an electric mixer, beat at high speed until light and fluffy:

- 6 ounces (1½ sticks) unsalted butter
- 1 cup granulated sugar
- ¾ cup light brown sugar, packed
- ½ cup cocoa powder

Add one at a time and beat on medium speed until well creamed:

- 3 extra-large eggs
- 1 teaspoon pure vanilla extract

On a piece of wax paper, sift together:

- 2¾ cups cake flour
- 2 teaspoons baking soda
- 1½ teaspoons salt

At low speed, add the dry ingredients to the butter mixture alternately with:

- 1½ cups buttermilk

Pour the batter into the prepared molds, filling each mold three-quarters full. Bake for 20 to 25 minutes, or until a cake tester inserted into the center of a cake comes out clean. Cool on a wire rack for 15 to 20 minutes before turning the cakes out of the pans or 5 to 10 minutes before removing the cupcakes from their pans.

c a r a m e l c a k e *

I am a sucker for caramel or anything in the caramel family: Dulce de Leche, butterscotch, caramel apples, caramel popcorn. So, whether caramel is drizzled all over ice cream, plated with a dessert, piped into a truffle, or made into a cake, I'll try it. And this cake is amazing. We added some butterscotch chips for even more yummy-ness. Now, if you happen to be a chocoholic, simply substitute mini chocolate chips for the butterscotch chips.

If you are making Nostalgic Nibbles (page 76), grease and flour 16 molds of three Twinkie pans. If you are making cupcakes, grease and flour the tops of three 6-mold muffin pans and line 16 of the molds with paper liners. If you are making the beach pail (see A Day at the Beach, page 128), grease and flour four 4-inch round cake pans. Preheat the oven to 350°F. Have all ingredients at room temperature.

In the bowl of an electric mixer, beat at high speed until light and fluffy:
- 6 ounces (1½ sticks) unsalted butter
- 1¼ cups light brown sugar, packed

Add slowly and beat on medium speed until fluffy:
- 3 extra-large eggs
- 1 teaspoon pure vanilla extract

On a piece of wax paper, sift together:
- 2½ cups cake flour
- 2 teaspoons baking powder
- ¼ teaspoon baking soda
- ½ teaspoon salt

At low speed, add the dry ingredients to the butter and egg mixture alternately with:
- 6 ounces (¾ cup) milk

Fold in:
- 3 ounces (¾ cup) butterscotch chips or mini chocolate chips

Fill each mold or liner three-quarters full. Bake for 18 to 20 minutes, or until golden, or 30 minutes for the 4-inch round cakes. The tops should spring back when lightly pressed. Cool on a wire rack for 5 to 10 minutes before removing the cupcakes from their pans or before turning the cakes out of their pans.

the big bang*

I first heard the term "Big Bang" during my high school biology class. The only way I was able to translate this immense and unfathomable happening was to capture it with paper and pencil. Years later I am still trying to visually encapsulate it. This is my edible glimpse of our galaxy. A rich chocolate truffle echoes the molten center of our planet while a crunchy exterior of encrusted pistachios will have you digging in for more. To top it all off, chaotic swirls of chocolate explode from the truffle.

WHAT YOU WILL NEED:

Cake
12 Pistachio Ganache Truffles (page 82)

Plating
Caramel Sauce (page 82)

Decoration
1 cup dark wafer chocolate, ½ cup white wafer chocolate, and two tablespoons ground pistachios to make 12 explosions of chocolate

Colors
yellow and orange candy color

Miscellaneous
one mini cheesecake pan, pastry cones, 1 half-sheet pan, parchment paper

HOW TO

1. Melt the dark wafer and white wafer chocolates separately. Using the Color Mixing Chart on pages 44—45, tint the white chocolate caramel. Pour the dark and caramel-colored chocolate into two separate pastry cones.

2. Line the half-sheet pan with parchment paper. Cut a medium hole in the dark chocolate pastry cone and pipe overlapping, random elliptical lines onto the parchment, keeping the design no more than 2 inches wide and 3 inches high. It is best if one end of the design is narrower to facilitate insertion into the truffle. Cut a medium hole in the caramel chocolate pastry cone and pipe it over the dark chocolate with a few sporadic elliptical lines. Before the chocolate sets sprinkle ground pistachios on top. Make 12 swirls in total. Set the designs aside to harden.

3. If desired, flip the designs and over-pipe additional caramel lines and sprinkle with pistachios.

4. Prepare the truffles and caramel sauce.

5. Before the ganache has completely set, press the chocolate designs ½ inch deep into the center of each truffle.

6. Plate the truffles on a bed of caramel sauce.

7. For fullest flavor, serve the cakes at room temperature.

pistachio ganache truffles*

This is one of the tastiest desserts the Bakehouse offers for Passover, a decadent treat from the rich ganache to the sea of caramel the truffle rests on. You would be hard-pressed to find a more perfect finale. Enjoy every bite.

You'll need one ungreased 12-mold mini cheesecake pan. Preheat the oven to 350°F.

CARAMEL SAUCE

This sauce is great paired not only with these truffles, but with ice cream, too. It keeps well in the refrigerator for at least a month.

In a heavy saucepan, melt:
- 4 ounces (1 stick) unsalted butter

Add and cook until amber colored, stirring occasionally:
- 1 cup sugar

Meanwhile, in a separate saucepan, over medium heat, scald:
- 1 cup heavy cream

When the sugar mixture is caramelized, slowly whisk in the heavy cream; be careful, because the sugar mixture will bubble up as the cream is added. Stir until smooth. Remove from the heat. Set aside.

CRUST

In a small bowl, combine:
- 1 cup finely ground pistachios
- ⅓ cup sugar
- 2 tablespoons plus 1 teaspoon melted unsalted butter

Place 2 tablespoons of crust into the bottom of each cheesecake mold. Press firmly onto the bottom and one third of the way up the sides. Bake for 5 to 10 minutes or until lightly browned. Set aside.

GANACHE

In a small bowl placed over a hot-water bath, melt:
- 6 ounces finely chopped semisweet chocolate

In a saucepan over medium heat, bring to a boil:
- ¾ cup heavy cream

Add the heavy cream to the chocolate and let sit for 3 minutes. Then whisk until the chocolate is melted and the ganache is smooth.

Pour the ganache into the crust molds. Chill until firm (approximately 2 hours). If you plan on making the Big Bang (page 80), before the ganache has completely set, press the chocolate designs ½ inch deep into the center of each truffle.

To unmold, push a wooden spoon through the pan openings under each mold. With a metal spatula, remove the metal bottom from each truffle. Store the ganache truffles in the refrigerator in an airtight container for up to 1 week. Remove the truffles from the refrigerator 2 hours before serving. Plate with the caramel sauce.

Whenever I mention cream puffs, my mom steps back in time to recount how her mother often served them with chocolate sauce; it was a family favorite. All of my mom's nine brothers and sisters delighted in the feast. I'm sure it wasn't easy to bake for a brood of ten, but Pâte à Choux is a simple recipe that makes it seem feasible.

I transformed the pâte à choux into little eggs sitting in birds' nests. Perfect for a baby shower or Easter, the nests are simply decorated with chocolate grass, a sprinkling of sliced almonds, and a dusting of confectioners' sugar.

Take care not to eat all of the cream-puff eggs before your guests arrive!

Cake

6 to 8 Pâte à Choux nests and 18 to 24 Pâte à
Choux eggs (page 85)

Filling

3 cups French Custard made from Pastry Cream
(page 86)

Decoration

½ cup dark wafer chocolate to make grass,
¼ cup sliced almonds

Tips

choose a star tip between #26 and #30, and a #6
or #7 round tip

Miscellaneous

pastry cones, 1 half-sheet pan, parchment
paper, six to eight 5-inch (or larger) bases,
confectioners' sugar

HOW TO

1. Prepare the Pastry Cream.

2. Prepare the Pâte à Choux nests and eggs.

3. Line the half-sheet pan with parchment paper. Melt the dark wafer chocolate and pour it into a pastry cone. Cut a medium hole in the cone and pipe semi-parallel lines, by moving the cone back and forth across the length of the sheet pan. Set aside to harden.

4. Prepare the French Custard.

5. With a small serrated knife, carefully trim off the over-piped portion of the nest and set aside. Adhere the bottom portion of the nest to its base with a dollop of French Custard.

6. Place the rest of the French Custard into a pastry bag with a coupler, and with the tip between #26 and #30, pipe a spiral to cover the bottom of the nest. Pipe extra French Custard on the outer edge. Place the trimmed edge back on top of the custard. Repeat with the remaining nests.

7. Change the tip to a #6 round tip. To fill the eggs, insert the pastry tip into the underside of each cream puff. Squeeze until the cream seeps out around the tip's edge or you feel the egg swell in your hand. Repeat with the remaining eggs.

8. Place 3 eggs in each nest. Finely dust with confectioners' sugar.

9. Break apart the chocolate into 3- to 4-inch strips and randomly place the segments into each nest. Sprinkle almonds over the tops of the nests.

10. Serve right away.

pâte à choux nests*

YIELD: 6 TO 8 NESTS AND 18 TO 24 EGGS

This classic French recipe is versatile enough to be used for sweet éclairs and cream puffs or as a shell for savory appetizers. Don't be intimidated by its French origins; it is so easy to make that all you need is a saucepan and a wooden spoon.

Trace six to eight 3½-inch circles onto a piece of parchment paper. Invert the parchment paper onto a sheet pan. Line an additional sheet pan with parchment paper. Preheat the oven to 350°F. Have all ingredients at room temperature.

In a saucepan over medium heat, bring to a boil:

- 1 cup milk
- 4 ounces (1 stick) unsalted butter, cut into slices
- Pinch of salt
- 1 teaspoon sugar

Turn the heat to medium and add:

- 1 cup all-purpose flour, sifted

Beat with a wooden spoon until the batter pulls away from the side of the pan and forms a ball.

Remove from the heat.

Beat in one at a time:

- 4 large eggs

Beat until glossy.

Place the dough, while it is still warm, into a pastry bag with a coupler and a #12 round tip. Using firm pressure and staying within the border of the template you traced, pipe out a 3½-inch circle and fill it in with a continuous spiral. The dough should be approximately ½-inch high. Pipe an additional circle on top of the first 3½-inch circle; it should be about ½ inch higher than the center spiral. Do not pipe an overlapping additional spiral. Make 6 to 8 nests in total. On a separate sheet pan, pipe 3 nickel-size balls (the eggs) per nest.

Bake the eggs for 20 to 25 minutes and the nests for 28 to 35 minutes, or until puffed and browned.

pastry cream **

YIELD: 1½ CUPS

Pastry cream is basically vanilla custard. Use it to fill cream puffs, éclairs, or fruit tarts, or lighten the texture by folding in whipped cream—thus making French Custard (see below). It holds up well when being piped, so it is perfect for our Cream Puff Nests. Prepare the Pastry Cream in advance, but do not fold in the whipped cream until you are ready to assemble the nests. Any leftover Pastry Cream can be made into a crème anglaise by thinning it out with cream.

In a saucepan over high heat, bring to a boil:
- 1 cup milk
- ¼ vanilla bean, sliced down one side (see Note)

In the bowl of an electric mixer on medium speed, beat until light and fluffy:
- 3 large egg yolks
- ⅓ cup sugar
- Pinch of salt

Add and mix to combine:
- 2 tablespoons cornstarch

Remove the vanilla bean from the milk. Scrape the seeds out with a small paring knife and put them back in the milk, discarding the bean. Slowly beat the hot milk into the yolk mixture and return the mixture to the saucepan. Bring it to a boil over medium-low heat, stirring constantly. Reduce the heat to low and continue boiling for 1 minute, stirring constantly.

Pour the pastry cream into a medium stainless-steel bowl, cover it with plastic wrap, and refrigerate until cold.

NOTE:

You can substitute ¾ teaspoon pure vanilla extract for the vanilla bean. Add the vanilla extract right at the end when the pastry cream is removed from the heat.

FRENCH CUSTARD

YIELD: 4½ CUPS FRENCH CUSTARD

For best results, we recommend preparing the French Custard right before serving or assembling your cakes.

Prepare the Pastry Cream as directed above.

In the bowl of an electric mixer fitted with a whisk attachment, whip until stiff:
- 1½ cups heavy cream
- 2 tablespoons confectioners' sugar
- ½ teaspoon pure vanilla extract

Stir the pastry cream until smooth. Fold in one quarter of the whipped cream and mix just until combined. Fold in the remaining whipped cream.

i scream, you scream...*

We all scream for ice cream! While browsing through our local Williams-Sonoma, I found these great ice-cream-cone pans, and I knew I would have to include them in the book. Even though I make cakes for a living, ice cream remains one of my favorite desserts, and mint chocolate chip is my favorite flavor. We topped our classic Pound Cake with a soft-serve spiral of mint chocolate chip cream. Feel free to create an ode to your favorite. How about a Pecan Pound Cake cone with a Whipped Chocolate Ganache (page 105) topping? Now that is very adult.

Dip the "ice cream" in sprinkles or try our hard Chocolate Shell. What fun.

Cake
12 Pound Cake ice cream cones (page 89)

Topping
Mint Chocolate Chip Cream (page 90)

Optional Topping
colored sprinkles (½ cup of sprinkles covers approximately 6 cones) or Chocolate Shell (page 91)

Tip
large #848 star

Miscellaneous
2 ice-cream-cone pans, pastry bag

HOW TO

1 Bake the cakes and let them cool completely. Trim the domes off and trim the bottoms to make sure the ice cream cones will not wobble when standing on their own.

2 Prepare the cream and other optional toppings.

3 Place the cream in the pastry bag with the star tip. Make sure the star tip's rays are as open as possible to allow the mini chips to pass through without clogging the tip.

4 Pipe a large circle on top of each cone, being careful to stay within the confines of the cone's top edge. Continue spiraling upward, getting narrower with each pass until tailing off with a flourish to create a point. Chill in the refrigerator or freezer for 1 to 2 hours or overnight in an airtight container. Remove 1 hour before serving. If adding additional toppings, see steps 5 to 7.

5 Freeze the filled cones until the mousse is hard to the touch, 1 to 2 hours.

6 Sprinkles: Place the colored sprinkles in a bowl large enough to accommodate a cone rolling in it. Roll each soft-serve portion of the frozen cone in the sprinkles, pressing the mousse firmly to adhere the sprinkles.

7 Glaze: Pour the Chocolate Shell into a tall, narrow container. Submerge one inverted cone at a time up to the cake line. Pull up and out while lightly spinning the cone to allow any excess glaze to drip off. Place right side up on a sheet pan to set. If necessary, dip the cone again once the first layer of Chocolate Shell has dried.

8 For the fullest flavor, serve the cakes at room temperature.

p o u n d   c a k e *

YIELD: 12 ICE CREAM CONES OR 3 MINI TIERED CAKES

···

Most of my mom's pound cakes have sour cream added in, but this classic comes from my sweet-toothed husband, Luiz. Since we reduced the recipe, we are just shy of the traditional "pound of sugar, pound of butter, pound of flour" pound cake. But, true to its name, it is dense, moist, and delicious.

If you are making I Scream, You Scream . . . (page 87), grease two 6-mold ice-cream-cone pans or mini tiered cake pans.

If you are making mini tiered cakes, grease two 2-inch, two 3-inch, and two 4-inch round cake pans.

Preheat the oven to 350°F. Have all ingredients at room temperature.

In the bowl of an electric mixer, cream well:
- 12 ounces (3 sticks) unsalted butter
- 1¾ cups sugar

Add and cream at high speed until light and fluffy:
- 7 extra-large egg yolks
- 1 teaspoon pure vanilla extract

On a piece of wax paper, sift together:
- 2½ cups all-purpose flour
- ½ teaspoon baking powder

Add the dry ingredients to the butter and egg mixture and mix on low speed just until combined.

In a clean bowl of an electric mixer with a whip attachment, whip until stiff but not dry:
- 5 extra-large egg whites

Fold one quarter of the egg whites into the batter until combined. Then gently fold in the remaining egg whites.

Pour the batter into the prepared pans, filling each three-quarters full. Bake for 28 to 30 minutes, or until a cake tester inserted into the center of a cake comes out clean. Cool on a wire rack for 15 to 20 minutes. Turn the cakes out of their pans. Invert to cool, so they are right side up. Slice off the dome that formed when baking.

mint chocolate chip cream*

YIELD: 6 CUPS

I still feel a bit childish going into an ice cream shop asking for my usual: "I'll have the mint on a sugar cone with"—spoken very quietly—"colored sprinkles." Now I can make my own version at home.

For best results we recommend preparing the Mint Chocolate Chip Cream right before serving or assembling your cakes.

In the bowl of an electric mixer fitted with a whisk attachment, whip until stiff:
- 3 cups heavy cream
- 5 tablespoons confectioners' sugar, sifted
- ½ teaspoon mint extract

Fold in:
- ¼ cup plus 1 tablespoon mini chocolate chips

CHOCOLATE SHELL *

Inspired by the Brown Bonnet served at the Carvel ice cream shops, and by all of the other old-fashioned ice cream dips, we made our soft-serve wafer cone complete with a dunk into our Chocolate Shell. Choose between milk chocolate or tinted white chocolate—both are sure to please.

This glaze is meant to cover frozen desserts. If the cream or cake is at room temperature or not cold enough, the glaze will drip off, melt the cream, or turn out semi-transparent. The glaze is meant to be used in a warm to hot liquid state, 98° to 105°F.

Any leftovers can be stored in an airtight container, at room temperature, for up to 1 month.

MILK CHOCOLATE SHELL

The ingredients can alternatively be melted in a double boiler.

YIELD: 1³/₄ CUPS
LIQUID GLAZE

In a glass bowl, combine and microwave at 30-second intervals, stirring in between, until melted (it should take approximately four passes in the microwave):

- 9⅓ ounces chopped milk chocolate
- 7 ounces (1 cup) vegetable shortening

If necessary, whisk to combine.

WHITE CHOCOLATE SHELL

The ingredients can alternatively be melted in a double boiler.

YIELD: 1³/₄ CUPS
LIQUID GLAZE

In a glass bowl, combine and microwave at 30-second intervals, stirring in between, until melted (it should take approximately four passes in the microwave):

- 10½ ounces chopped white chocolate
- 5¼ ounces (¾ cup) vegetable shortening

To tint the glaze, stir in:

- 6 drops red candy color

If necessary, whisk to combine.

make a wish cupcakes*

The Bakehouse's signature cake is our Mini Birthday Cake, and although we taught everyone how to make it in our first book, I was sad not to see it represented in our Little Cakes book, since it was one of the first little cakes I ever made. A batch of fifteen 4-inch cakes brightened up our storefront way back in 1996, and everything began to change. This time around I am offering a variation on the original, which I designed on a whim: Make a Wish Cupcakes. These cupcakes use some of the same piping techniques as the original, and they too have edible chocolate candles, and a colorful palette.

The directions below illustrate how to make a cupcake with purple icing, green and teal piping, and a pink candle. Substitute whatever colors match your party.

Cake
12 Classic Vanilla Cupcakes (page 95)

Icing
House Buttercream (page 31) or Kaye's Buttercream (with a pastel palette) (page 32) or Kids' Buttercream (page 33)

Optional filling
Goodies and Cream made with shaved chocolate (page 98)

Decoration
1 cup white wafer chocolate to make 12 candles

Colors
Choose three liquid gel colors from the following list: purple, teal, green, yellow, blue, violet, neon pink, and orange. Choose one candy color plus yellow from the following list: neon bright pink, green, blue, or violet

Tips
#16 Ateco and/or #27 P&H star tip

Miscellaneous
one 12-mold muffin pan, 2 pastry bags, 2 couplers, pastry cones, 1 half-sheet pan, parchment paper or cellophane

1 Bake the cupcakes and let them cool completely. Freeze for 1 hour to overnight.

2 Prepare the icing and optional filling.

3 Fill the cupcakes as directed in Filling a Cupcake, number 2 or number 3, on page 22. Chill for at least 30 minutes or overnight.

4 Melt the white wafer chocolate. Using the Color Mixing Chart on pages 44—45, tint ⅛ cup yellow and ⅜ cup neon pink. Pour the chocolates into two separate pastry cones and cut a medium-size hole in each. On the sheet pan lined with parchment paper pipe out twelve 3-inch candles (see Adventurous Alternative). They should be at least ¼ inch wide and ⅛ inch thick. Set aside to harden.

5 When the chocolate has set, pipe yellow flames on the top of each candle. Set aside to harden. When the flames have set, flip the candles over and pipe flames on the opposite side. This way the flame can be seen from both sides of the candle.

6 Prepare the colored buttercream: approximately 1½ cups purple for the base, 1 cup neon green for the shell borders, and ½ cup teal for the rosettes.

7 Ice the cupcakes with a smooth finish as directed on page 26.

8 Place the neon green buttercream into a pastry bag with a coupler, and with a star tip pipe a shell border around the top edge of each cupcake. See the piping techniques below.

9 Place the teal buttercream in a pastry bag with a coupler, and with a star tip pipe a rosette in the center of each cupcake.

10 Stick the candles into the rosettes, pressing them halfway down into each cupcake.

11 For fullest flavor, serve the cakes at room temperature.

ADVENTUROUS ALTERNATIVE

Cut 6 drinking straws down one side. Pipe melted and tinted chocolate into the straws, gently tapping them to release any air bubbles as you go, until the straws are full. Set aside to harden. When the chocolate has set, carefully remove the plastic straws to reveal solid chocolate cylinders. With a paring knife, score the cylinders every 3 inches. Break the cylinders along these score marks. Pipe a yellow flame on the top of each cylinder and set aside to harden.

PIPING TECHNIQUES

Shell Border
  • Star tip (#16)

Hold the bag at a 45-degree angle to the cake surface. Rest the tip where you are going to begin piping the shell. Without moving the pastry bag, apply a heavy, consistent pressure, allowing the tip to rise as the icing builds. Once the shell has formed, decrease the pressure while dragging the tip downward, forming a tail. Begin the next shell overlapping the preceding tail.

Rosettes
  • Star Tip (# 27)

Hold the bag perpendicular to the surface of the cake. Using consistent pressure, pipe a tight circle. Without releasing the pressure, continue the spiral over the first circle, releasing the pressure as you tail it off.

classic vanilla cupcakes *

YIELD: 12 CUPCAKES

Our Classic Vanilla Cupcake has a nostalgic flavor and is wonderful paired with vanilla buttercream or fudge. It is also delicious glazed, left plain, or even cut in half and served with fresh fruit and a dollop of whipped cream.

Grease the top of a 12-mold muffin pan and line it with paper liners. Preheat the oven to 350°F. Have all ingredients at room temperature.

Sift into a mixing bowl:
- 1¾ cups plus 2 tablespoons cake flour
- ¾ teaspoon salt

Add and mix to combine:
- 1 cup sugar

Add:
- ½ cup plus 2½ teaspoons warmed milk (110°F)
- 2 large eggs
- 4 ounces (1 stick) very soft unsalted butter
- ½ teaspoon pure vanilla extract

Beat at low speed with a whisk attachment for 1 minute. Scrape down the bowl. Raise the speed to medium-low and beat for 1½ minutes.

Add:
- 1½ teaspoons baking powder

Mix at low speed for 30 seconds.

Scoop the batter into the prepared molds, filling each three-quarters full. Bake for 18 to 20 minutes, or until golden.

The tops should spring back when lightly pressed. Cool on a wire rack for 5 to 10 minutes before removing the cupcakes from the pan.

halloween cupcakes **

Halloween is my favorite holiday, perhaps because it is so visual—from the costumes to the treats. I also love the fact that the chance to be creative and daring is welcomed.

We sell more than a thousand of these spooky cupcakes every Halloween. With twenty designs to choose from including ghosts, skeletons, gravestones, and mummies, you won't know which to make—so why not try them all? The cupcakes are devil's food (how appropriate) and all of the decorations are made with chocolate. A simple decorating alternative that most kids will love is to encrust the top of these cupcakes with small candies such as M&Ms or Sno Caps. Any leftover candy can be handed out to the trick-or-treaters.

When your favorite holiday rolls around, use the same Chocolate Method techniques to decorate your cupcakes: for Christmas make chocolate reindeer, Santa hats, stockings, and candy canes and for Easter make chocolate Easter baskets, bunnies, and eggs.

Cake

18 Devil's Food cupcakes (page 78)

Icing

Kids' Buttercream (page 33) or Matt's Fudge Icing (page 35)

Optional Filling

Goodies and Cream made with crushed Butterfingers or Heath bars (page 98)

Decoration

The amounts of chocolate may differ depending on your chosen design. To be on the safe side, have approximately 2 cups of dark and 3 cups of white wafer chocolate on hand, along with sprinkles or nonpareils for cupcake edging.

Colors

blue, orange, yellow, green, and purple liquid gel colors and orange, red, blue, green, yellow, and purple candy color. Choose colors according to what's appropriate for your design.

Miscellaneous

three 6-mold muffin pans, pastry cones, Halloween templates (pages 171–172), 1 half-sheet pan, parchment paper or cellophane

HOW TO

1. Bake the cupcakes and let them cool completely. Freeze for 1 hour to overnight.

2. Prepare the icing of your choice.

3. Melt the dark wafer and white wafer chocolates separately. Using the templates provided, make 18 Halloween designs as illustrated in The Chocolate Method (pages 40–43). Here are sample chocolate amounts: to make 18 jack-o'-lanterns melt 2²/₃ cups white wafer chocolate and ¼ cup dark wafer chocolate. Tint the white chocolate: tint approximately 1 cup of it orange, 3 tablespoons yellow, and 3 tablespoons green. To make 18 ghosts, melt 1½ cups of white wafer chocolate and ⅛ cup of dark wafer chocolate. To make the hand in a pool of blood, melt 5 cups of white wafer chocolate and ¼ cup of dark wafer chocolate. Tint half the white chocolate red and the other half neon green. Set aside the completed designs to harden. For all other designs, use the photograph as a color guide and melt and tint chocolate accordingly. The base colors will need the most chocolate, while the details will need less.

4. Fill the cupcakes as directed in Filling a Cupcake, number 2 or number 3, on page 22. Chill for at least 30 minutes.

5. Ice the cupcakes with an old-fashioned or flat icing as directed on pages 25 and 26.

6. Put a dollop of icing on the underside of each design and place it right side up on the cupcake. If the design is freestanding, press it halfway into the cupcake.

7. Add any over-piping such as dots, grass, stars, or dirt with the remaining chocolate.

8. For fullest flavor, serve the cakes at room temperature.

goodies and cream filling*

YIELD: 2½ CUPS

Originally we added crushed Oreos to a whipped-cream base to create one of the simplest and best-tasting fillings around. Since then we have found many goodies that can be crushed and added to create a variety of flavors. At Halloween we make an awesome candy bar mousse by crushing Heath bars and Butterfingers and folding them into our whipped-cream base. Add graham crackers for a touch of s'mores flavor, or for a more refined palate simply take your favorite chocolate (chilled) and grate it into the whipped cream. This provides a bit of crunch and a lot of flavor!

For best results, we recommend preparing the Goodies and Cream right before serving or assembling your cupcakes.

NOTE:

If you plan on piping this filling, make sure the add-ins are finely ground so they do not get clogged in the pastry bag.

In the bowl of an electric mixer fitted with a whisk attachment, whip until stiff:

- 1¼ cups heavy cream
- 2 tablespoons confectioners' sugar
- ¼ teaspoon pure vanilla extract

Gently fold in:

- ½ cup of your favorite crushed goody

mini acorn cupcakes**

Fun for children and adults alike, these bite-size cupcakes are a twist on their larger cousin. If you have embraced little plates and tasting menus, consider having dessert tapas. Make three or more different cakes in these bite-size portions; then plate, serve, and watch your guests swoon. On a similar note, if you are planning a brunch, fill a basket with a variety of mini muffins.

Here we ice our Chocolate Coconut Cupcakes with a dollop of German Chocolate Icing—sinfully delicious. If the mood strikes you, top the icing with a chocolate acorn.

WHAT YOU WILL NEED:

Cake
40 miniature Chocolate Coconut Cupcakes (page 100)

Icing
German Chocolate Icing (page 101)

Decoration
2 cups white wafer chocolate and ½ cup dark wafer chocolate to make 40 acorns

Colors
Yellow and orange candy color

Miscellaneous
2 mini muffin pans, pastry cones, acorn templates (page 170), 1 half-sheet pan, parchment paper or cellophane

HOW TO

1. Prepare the German Chocolate Icing.

2. Bake the cupcakes and let them cool completely. Freeze for 1 hour or overnight.

3. Melt the dark wafer and white wafer chocolates separately. Set aside 2 tablespoons white chocolate for highlights. Tint the remaining white chocolate light brown and dark brown. To make the light brown, mix together approximately ½ cup white chocolate, ½ teaspoon dark chocolate, and 1 drop each of yellow and orange candy color. To make dark brown, mix together approximately ½ cup white chocolate, 1 tablespoon dark chocolate, and 2 drops of orange candy color. Using the templates provided, make 40 acorn tops and 40 acorn bottoms as illustrated in The Chocolate Method (pages 40–43).

4. When the chocolate has set, adhere the top of the acorn to the bottom with a dot of melted chocolate (any leftover chocolate will do, as this dot will not be seen). Hold in place for 10 seconds until set.

5. Ice the cupcakes as directed in Old-Fashioned Icing on a Cupcake, page 25.

6. Place one acorn on the top of each cupcake.

7. For fullest flavor, serve the cakes at room temperature.

chocolate coconut cupcakes with german chocolate icing*

YIELD: 40 MINI CUPCAKES

Instead of the classic milk chocolate cake usually paired with German chocolate icing, we went over the top and made a chocolate coconut cake. In addition, unlike the traditional icing, which has unpredictable results, our simple and irresistible icing is made with sweetened condensed milk, toasted coconut, and pecans.

Grease the tops of two 24-mold mini muffin pans and line 40 molds with mini paper liners (optional). If not using paper liners, grease the molds as well. Preheat the oven to 350°F. Have all ingredients at room temperature.

In the bowl of an electric mixer, beat at high speed until light and fluffy:
- 6 ounces (1½ sticks) unsalted butter
- 1 cup sugar

Add, one at a time, and beat on medium speed until fluffy:
- 3 large eggs

Add and beat just to combine:
- 1 teaspoon pure vanilla extract

On a piece of wax paper, sift together:
- 1 cup all-purpose flour
- ½ cup cocoa powder
- ½ teaspoon baking soda
- ¼ teaspoon salt

At low speed, add the dry ingredients to the butter and egg mixture alternately with:
- ½ cup buttermilk

Fold in:
- 1 cup toasted sweetened coconut

Fill each liner or mold three-quarters full. Bake 15 to 17 minutes, or until a cake tester inserted into the center of a cupcake comes out clean. The tops should spring back when lightly touched. Cool on a wire rack for 5 to 10 minutes before removing the cupcakes from the pans.

Spread with German Chocolate Icing (see opposite).

DULCE DE LECHE *

My Brazilian husband, Luiz, was the first to introduce me to this sweeter-than-sweet delicacy. Now I see it everywhere: in ice cream, as a filling for churros, or in cheesecake. Personally, I like it best out of the can.

The classic, and Brazilian, way of preparing this delicacy is to boil a can of sweetened condensed milk. There are rumors that the can can explode, although I have never heard of a case firsthand. But please take care and follow the directions carefully. As an alternative, you can buy cans of dulce de leche that have already been cooked. They aren't as easy to find, but we recommend looking in the Latin section of your grocery store. In addition, we are giving stovetop and oven directions.

Boiling directions:

Place one 14-ounce unopened can of sweetened condensed milk in a deep saucepan. Cover with water. Bring to a boil. **You must make sure that the can is always totally covered with water.** Reduce the heat to low and simmer, adding more water as necessary to keep the can covered. Simmer for 2 hours.

Using tongs, carefully remove the can from the water or let it sit in the water bath until it reaches room temperature. Once it has reached room temperature, the can can be refrigerated to speed up the cooling process. The can must be permitted to **cool down completely before opening** to avoid any danger of explosion and/or burn injuries.

Stovetop directions:

Pour one 14-ounce can sweetened condensed milk into the top of a double boiler. Over low heat, simmer for 1 to 1½ hours or until thick and caramel-colored, stirring occasionally.

Oven directions:

Pour one 14-ounce can sweetened condensed milk into a 9-inch pie plate. Cover the plate with aluminum foil. Place the pie plate in a larger shallow pan. Fill the larger pan with hot water. Bake at 425ºF for 1 hour or until thick and caramel-colored. With a whisk or in the bowl of an electric mixer, beat until smooth.

GERMAN CHOCOLATE ICING *

Like candy, this thick and gooey icing is so sweet and good you just can't stop devouring it.

Mix together:
- 1 recipe Dulce de Leche (above)
- ¾ cup chopped toasted pecans (see Note)
- ¾ cup toasted sweetened coconut (see Note)

NOTE:

To toast pecans and coconut, place on an ungreased sheet pan. Bake at 350ºF for 12 to 15 minutes, or until fragrant. Let cool.

The rather serious meringue cake takes a wild turn when it is decorated with faux animal prints. The leopard spots and zebra and tiger stripes are made with chocolate. Vary the base color according to which animal print you want to make: coffee for the leopard, white for the zebra, and orange for the tiger.

WHAT YOU WILL NEED:

Cake
sixteen 3½-inch Crisp Meringues to make 4 Wild Meringue cakes (page 104)

Filling
1 cup Whipped Chocolate Ganache (page 105) and 1 cup Whipped Cream (page 35)

Icing
Kaye's Buttercream (page 32)

Decoration
for 4 cakes decorated with zebra or tiger stripes, 1 cup dark wafer chocolate; for 4 cakes decorated with leopard spots, ⅔ cup white wafer chocolate and 1 cup dark wafer chocolate

Colors
yellow and orange candy color, yellow and orange liquid gel color

Miscellaneous
3 half-sheet pans, four 3¾-inch cardboard or thick grease-proof paper rounds, pastry cones, parchment paper, turntable, four 6-inch (or larger) bases

1. Prepare the chocolate ganache and buttercream. Refrigerate the ganache until you are ready to assemble the meringues. The buttercream can be stored in an airtight container at room temperature for up to 3 days. If making the zebra, reserve 1½ cups buttercream. Flavor the remaining buttercream with coffee (see page 33). Flavor all of the buttercream with coffee if making leopard or tiger cakes.

2. Prepare the meringues. Let cool (once cool, assemble the meringue cakes right away or they will lose their crispness).

3. Meanwhile, melt the dark wafer and/or white wafer chocolates separately. If making tiger or zebra stripes, draw a guide: on a piece of parchment paper draw 2 parallel lines 4 inches apart. Pour the chocolate into a pastry cone and cut a medium-size hole in the tip. On a sheet pan lined with parchment paper, with the guide underneath, pipe out tiger/zebra stripes running between the two lines, staying within the guidelines. They should be at least ⅛ inch thick and between 2 and 4 inches long. If making leopard spots, tint the white chocolate light brown (see the Color Mixing Chart on pages 44–45). Pour the chocolates into separate pastry cones and first pipe out dark chocolate irregular outlines, then fill in with caramel (refer to the photograph). Set aside to harden.

4. Prepare 1 cup of Whipped Cream. Whip 1 generous cup of the chocolate ganache. Remix the buttercream to get out any air and lumps.

5. To fill the meringues: There are 16 meringues in total. Place 4 of the meringues, flat side down, onto four 3¾-inch cardboard rounds, adhering them with a dot of coffee buttercream. Spread a thin layer of buttercream on top of each of these meringues. Divide the whipped cream evenly among the four meringues, spreading to make level. Next, spread a thin layer of coffee buttercream on the tops of the remaining 12 meringues. Place one layer of meringue (from the 12), flat and un-iced side up, on top of the whipped cream layers. Spread a thin layer of coffee buttercream on the flat and un-iced side and stack another meringue flat side down. Divide the whipped chocolate ganache evenly among the 4 cakes, spreading to make level. Top off with a final layer of meringue, flat side up. Place in the freezer for 30 minutes to firm up.

6. Crumb-coat the cakes with coffee buttercream as directed on page 24. Chill.

7. Prepare the final coat of buttercream: coffee buttercream with 1 drop each of orange and yellow liquid gel for the leopard fur, reserved untinted Kaye's Buttercream for the zebra, or coffee buttercream with 3 drops of orange liquid gel for the tiger fur.

8. Adhere the cardboard round supporting the cakes to their bases.

9. Score the chocolate zebra and tiger stripes accordingly, cutting some to the height of the cake, some shorter. Stick the chocolate designs randomly around the cakes.

10. Place any remaining buttercream into a pastry cone. Cut a large hole in the tip and pipe a wavy line border around the bottom edge of the cakes.

11. Serve the cakes at room temperature, chilled, or frozen.

crisp meringues**

Before my husband studied computers and business, he worked at a French bakery. A rather sedate version of our Wild Meringues was one of their best sellers (their cake was simply encrusted with toasted almonds), and the Bakehouse has embraced it, selling out every Passover. The meringues are delicious served at room temperature or as a frozen dessert in the summer; both melt in your mouth.

Trace eight 3½-inch circles onto two pieces of parchment paper. Invert the parchment papers onto two separate sheet pans. Preheat the oven to 250°F. Have all ingredients at room temperature.

In a food processor, finely grind:
- 1¼ cups sliced almonds
- 1 tablespoon cornstarch
- 2 tablespoons sugar

In the bowl of an electric mixer, whip until frothy:
- 6 large egg whites

Gradually add, and beat until very stiff:
- ¾ cup sugar
- ¼ teaspoon cream of tartar

Fold the nut mixture into the egg mixture with:
- ⅛ teaspoon almond extract
- 1 teaspoon pure vanilla extract

Gently place the meringue into a pastry bag with a #805 tip. Pipe out sixteen 3½-inch circles, filling in each circle with a spiral into the center. Bake for 2½ hours, or until totally crisp. Fill and assemble the meringues immediately so they do not lose their crispness (see directions on page 103).

whipped chocolate ganache*

YIELD: 4 3/4 CUPS OF FILLING WHEN WHIPPED

If you are looking for a filling or topping for your cake but don't want to be overwhelmed by sweetness, try this ganache. No sugar is added to the semisweet chocolate, so the true chocolate essence comes through. The recipe is simple to make, whips up easily, and tastes delicious. Unwhipped, it will stay fresh for 2 weeks in your refrigerator.

In a double boiler or in a medium metal bowl placed over a hot-water bath, melt:

- 8 ounces chopped semisweet chocolate

In a small saucepan, heat over medium-high heat:

- 1 quart heavy cream

Whisk one third of the cream into the chocolate until smooth. Slowly whisk in the remaining cream.

Refrigerate overnight or freeze for a few hours.

Whip until stiff.

These little gifts are subdued yet playful. A rich and elegant chocolate glaze unexpectedly tops a Peanut Butter Brownie. To add an extra punch of flavor, we first crumbed the brownies with a thin layer of Peanut Butter Icing.

The bows adorning the gifts are made with white chocolate "plastic." Top your precious gifts with a classic bow, Jorge's birthday bow, or a rosebud (see below).

WHAT YOU WILL NEED:

Cake
9 square Peanut Butter Brownie Cakes (page 108)

Icing
Peanut Butter Icing (page 34) and Chocolate Glaze (page 34)

Decoration
white Chocolate Plastic (page 109) ribbons and ¼ cup buttercream for piping patterns (optional)

Miscellaneous
one 12-mold square mini cake pan, ½ cup cornstarch for dusting, rolling pin, pastry cones (optional), wire rack for glazing, nine 4-inch (or larger) serving plates or bases

1. Prepare the white Chocolate Plastic. Bake the cakes and let them cool completely. Freeze for 1 hour to overnight.

2. Prepare the Peanut Butter Icing and Chocolate Glaze.

3. Crumb-coat the cakes with a thin layer of Peanut Butter Icing. Freeze for 30 minutes.

4. Glaze the cakes as directed on page 29. With an offset metal spatula, carefully place each cake onto its serving plate or base. Chill for 15 minutes.

5. Optional: Place ¼ cup of buttercream in a pastry cone and pipe out a delicate pattern of your choice onto the glaze or use the photographs as a guide.

6. Dust a clean, flat surface with cornstarch. With a rolling pin, roll out half of the white Chocolate Plastic to 1/16 inch thick (keep the remaining chocolate wrapped tightly in plastic wrap to prevent it from drying out). Cut it into ⅓ x 5-inch strips. Starting at the base of one side, place a strip down on the cake, carefully draping it over the top and then down the opposite side. Cut off any extra plastic by pressing a knife into the base of the cake. Repeat the process with another strip on the adjacent side so the ribbons cross in the center.

7. To make a classic bow (opposite, at right): Roll out the remaining chocolate plastic to 1/16 inch thick. Cut a ⅓ x 4-inch strip. Mark the center point. Gently curl the outer ends so they meet at the center. Press them together at the center and form two loops. Cut a 1¼-inch strip and wrap it around the center of the bow, so that the seam is on the underside. Cut two 1½-inch ribbon tails, trimming their ends at an angle, and place them down at a diagonal to the crossed ribbons. Place the bow on top.

8. To make Jorge's birthday bow (opposite, at left): Roll out the remaining chocolate plastic to 1/16 inch thick. Cut nineteen ⅓ x 2-inch strips. Curl each strip so their ends meet. Press the ends together and form a loop. Arrange 8 loops in a circle so that the ends meet in the center. Press together. Arrange 6 loops in a tight circle within the first circle, pressing gently to adhere at the center. For the next row, arrange 4 loops close together in the center of the bow. Lastly, place one loop on top. Carefully place the bow on top of the cake.

9. To make a rosebud (opposite, center): Roll out the remaining chocolate plastic to 1/16 inch thick. Cut a 2½ x ¾-inch strip. From this strip, cut out an arc along one length with the apex remaining ¾ inch. Starting at one point, roll the plastic tightly into a coil along the straight edge. When complete, flare some of the petals outward. Cut out two small leaves. Place the bud in the center of the cake with one leaf on each side.

10. For fullest flavor, serve the cakes at room temperature.

peanut butter brownie cakes*

Don't let the name fool you; these Peanut Butter Brownie Cakes are a serious dessert. Our little gifts to you are so dense, rich, and moist you will think you are feasting on chocolate truffles.

Grease and flour 9 molds of a 12-mold mini square pan. Preheat the oven to 350°F. Have all ingredients at room temperature.

In a saucepan over low heat, melt, whisking often:

- 3 ounces chopped unsweetened chocolate
- 8 ounces chopped semisweet chocolate
- 3 ounces (¾ stick) unsalted butter
- ½ cup crunchy peanut butter

Remove from the heat and set aside.

In the bowl of an electric mixer, beat at high speed until light and fluffy:

- 3 large eggs
- 1 cup sugar
- 2 teaspoons pure vanilla extract

Fold the chocolate mixture into the egg mixture, mixing only until combined.

On a piece of wax paper, sift together:

- ½ cup all-purpose flour
- ½ teaspoon baking powder
- ½ teaspoon salt

On low speed, add the dry ingredients to the batter and beat until combined.

Stir in by hand:

- 1 cup semisweet chocolate chips

Pour the batter into the prepared molds, filling the molds three-quarters full. Bake for 17 to 20 minutes, or until almost set. Cool on a wire rack for 15 to 20 minutes before turning the cakes out of the pans.

chocolate plastic*

Chocolate Plastic is a versatile and fun medium to work with. We made the bows that top our Little Gifts with it (page 106) but you can also make sculpted flowers from it much like you can with gum paste. You can even cover a cake with Chocolate Plastic, and it tastes much better than fondant. We used white chocolate, but in this recipe you can substitute dark, milk, or even wafer chocolate.

In a glass bowl, place in a microwave:
- 7 ounces chopped white chocolate

Melt the chocolate at 30-second intervals (approximately 3 passes in the microwave), stirring in between.

Add, stirring quickly just to combine:
- ¼ cup light corn syrup

Remove the chocolate plastic from the bowl and wrap it tightly in plastic wrap. Let the chocolate plastic set for a few hours or overnight at room temperature, or for 1 hour in the freezer.

When ready to roll out the plastic, dust a clean, flat surface with cornstarch. Knead the dough with your hands to make it smooth and malleable. If the dough is too hard to work, soften it in the microwave for 4 to 5 seconds and knead again. Roll the dough out to ¼ to ¹⁄₁₆ inch, depending on the design. Do not let the plastic sit out unwrapped because it will harden and become unworkable. When working with plastic, if necessary use dabs of water to adhere one piece to another.

be mine cakes *

Do you have a hot date for Valentine's Day? Well, try this cake as a gift to warm up the atmosphere. Or maybe for Mother's Day give one to Mom, one to your mother-in-law, and one to any mother important in your life. Even for a little girl's birthday, these cakes would be a giggly hit—just omit the spices and change the palette to light pinks and purples instead of the flaming reds and neons. Or go for that red-hot look and glaze the hearts with red-tinted white chocolate glaze.

Cake
12 spicy chocolate heart cakes (see page 112)

Filling
Cinnamon Chocolate Whipped Cream (page 113)

Icing
Chocolate Glaze (page 34)

Decoration
2½ cups white wafer chocolate to make 12 hearts and for drizzling, ¾ cup chocolate shavings or sprinkles (optional)

Colors
red and pink candy color

Miscellaneous
one scalloped mini heart pan, pastry cones, heart templates (page 169), 1 half-sheet pan, parchment paper or cellophane, wire rack for glazing

. . . .

HOW TO

. . . .

1. Bake the heart cakes and let them cool completely. Freeze for 1 hour or overnight.

2. Prepare the glaze.

3. Melt the white wafer chocolate and divide it equally among 3 bowls. Using the Color Mixing Chart on pages 44—45, tint one bowl pale pink, one bowl red, and one bowl neon pink. Pour the colored chocolates into 3 separate pastry cones. Cut small to medium holes in each.

4. Using the templates provided, make 12 hearts as illustrated in The Chocolate Method (pages 40—43). Set aside to harden. Save the remaining chocolate for drizzling. When needed, remelt the chocolate in a microwave or on the sheet pan over a hot-water bath.

5. Prepare the filling. Scoop approximately 1 tablespoon of filling into the indentation

in each heart. With a small metal spatula, spread the filling so it's flat and flush with the top surface of the cake. Freeze for 30 minutes or until the filling has set.

6. Glaze the cakes as directed on page 29.

7. Drizzle colored chocolate over the top of each cake until you are satisfied with the spattering effect.

8. Place a chocolate heart on the top of each heart cake; if it doesn't stick, squeeze a drop of melted chocolate under the heart to adhere it.

9. If desired, press chocolate shavings or sprinkles around the bottom of each cake before plating.

10. For fullest flavor, serve the cakes at room temperature.

spicy chocolate cakes*

I was trying to think of a new flavor for a cake and I knew my mom had long been trying to combine cinnamon and chocolate. Ding! I had an idea: not just cinnamon, but something fiery. Think Red-Hots meet chocolate: daring, spicy, and unexpectedly tempting.

Grease two 6-mold scalloped mini heart pans. Preheat the oven to 350°F. Have all ingredients at room temperature.

In a medium bowl, combine and whisk until smooth:

- 1 cup cocoa powder
- 1 cup hot water

Add and whisk until melted:

- 2 ounces chopped semisweet chocolate

Add and mix until smooth:

- 1/3 cup sour cream
- 1/2 teaspoon pure vanilla extract

In the bowl of an electric mixer, beat at high speed until light and fluffy:

- 8 ounces (2 sticks) unsalted butter
- 1 cup granulated sugar
- 1/3 cup light brown sugar, packed

Add one at a time and beat on medium speed until well creamed:

- 3 large eggs

On a piece of wax paper, sift together:

- 1¾ cups cake flour
- 1½ teaspoons baking soda
- ¼ teaspoon salt
- 2½ teaspoons ground cinnamon
- ¾ teaspoon cayenne pepper

At low speed, add the dry ingredients to the butter mixture alternately with the chocolate mixture, mixing until smooth.

Fill each heart three-quarters full with batter. Bake for 28 to 32 minutes, or until a cake tester inserted into the center of a cake comes out clean. Cool on a wire rack for 15 to 20 minutes before turning the cakes out of the pans.

cinnamon chocolate whipped cream*

YIELD: 1 CUP

Our Cinnamon Chocolate Whipped Cream can fill and ice the Spicy Chocolate Cake, opposite, but it is also delicious spooned onto pumpkin pie.

For best results we recommend preparing the whipped cream right before serving or assembling your cakes. Any leftovers can be stored in an airtight container in the refrigerator for up to 2 days. The whipped cream will break down as it sits in the refrigerator, so rewhip it in the bowl of an electric mixer for 1 minute or until medium to stiff peaks form.

In a glass bowl, melt in a microwave:
- 2 tablespoons finely chopped semisweet chocolate

Let the chocolate come to body temperature.

Meanwhile, in the bowl of an electric mixer fitted with a whisk attachment, whip until slightly thickened:
- ½ cup heavy cream
- 1 tablespoon confectioners' sugar
- Pinch of ground cinnamon

Add the chocolate and continue whipping at high speed until stiff.

caramel popcorn
cupcakes***

Are you having a sleepover birthday party? An Oscar bash? Or just a movie marathon? Why not serve these little popcorn cupcakes.

Wanting to imitate an old-fashioned popcorn box, I searched for red and white striped cupcake papers to no avail. So, I decided to make a striped chocolate shell to hold the cupcake instead. I piped buttercream "popcorn"—definitely more filling than the real thing, but very fun. An extra sweet surprise awaits you at the bottom of the shell (if you get that far): dulce de leche.

Cake
14 caramel cupcakes (see page 79)

Icing
Kaye's Buttercream (page 32) or House Buttercream (page 31)

Filling
Dulce de Leche (page 101)

Decoration
3½ cups white wafer chocolate to make 14 chocolate boxes

Colors
yellow liquid gel color and red candy color

Tip
#8 or #10 round

Miscellaneous
three 6-mold muffin pans, pastry bag, coupler, pastry cones, 6 to 12 silicone cupcake liners

HOW TO

1. Bake the cakes and let them cool completely. Freeze for 1 hour to overnight. Prepare the filling and icing.

2. Rest the silicone cupcake liners in a cupcake pan so that they are slightly flared at the top and do not touch the bottom.

3. Melt the white wafer chocolate. Pour one third of the chocolate into a bowl and tint it red. Pour the white and red chocolate into separate pastry cones and cut medium holes in the tip of each. Pipe alternating red and white stripes up the inside of each liner, using the ridges of the liner as a guide. Do not pipe any chocolate in the bottom of the liner until the chocolate has set on the sides; it may get filled as the chocolate settles. Let the chocolate set for a few minutes. Pipe an additional line of white chocolate around the top inner edge to give support, and fill in any areas where the cupcake liner is still visible. Set aside to harden (approximately 1 hour).

4. Carefully peel the silicone liner off the popcorn bucket.

5. Remove the cupcakes from the freezer.

6. Place 1½ tablespoons of dulce de leche in the bottom of each bucket. Place one cupcake, with the paper liner removed, into each bucket, trimming the bottom of the cupcake at an angle if necessary.

7. Prepare the tinted and flavored buttercream: approximately 2 tablespoons soft buttery yellow and 2 tablespoons dulce de leche buttercream (see page 33).

8. Place a coupler inside a pastry bag. With a metal spatula, spread a very small amount of the dulce de leche buttercream up one side of a pastry bag. Spread a very small amount of yellow adjacent to the dulce de leche. Fill the rest of the bag with the untinted buttercream. With a #8 or #10 round tip, pipe popcorn all over the top of the cupcake by squeezing and holding in place until a ball forms. Tail off. Then squeeze with fluctuating pressure as you move the tip up and down along half to three quarters of the ball's circumference.

9. For fullest flavor, serve the cakes at room temperature.

constructed cupcakes**

I never noticed the vast array of trucks, cars, and construction vehicles on the road until my son, Kase, was born. Anything with wheels calls for his attention. When he saw this construction site he wanted to dig in—not just eat, but play, too.

What makes these cupcakes unique is how they are assembled and decorated to look like a cake. Your guests can just reach for a cupcake and pull it apart from the rest—easier than slicing a cake!

Cake
18 Classic Chocolate Cupcakes to make 1 pull-apart cake (page 118)

Icing
one and a half recipes of Matt's Fudge Icing (page 35)

Decoration
⅛ cup dark wafer chocolate and 1½ cups white wafer chocolate to make 5 construction vehicles; cookie crumbs and candy

Tip
#12 round tip

Colors
orange, blue, yellow, and black candy color

Miscellaneous
three 6-mold muffin pans, pastry cones, vehicle templates (page 173), 1 half-sheet pan, parchment paper or cellophane, 16-inch square base (or larger)

HOW TO

1. Bake the cupcakes and let them cool completely. Freeze for 1 hour to overnight.

2. Prepare the fudge icing.

3. Melt the dark wafer and white wafer chocolates separately. Set aside 2 tablespoons of white chocolate. Using the Color Mixing Chart on pages 44—45, tint the white chocolate: approximately 2 tablespoons each of yellow, orange, royal blue, light blue, and gray. Using the templates provided, make 5 construction vehicles as illustrated in The Chocolate Method (pages 40—43). Extend the wheels of each vehicle with a ¼-inch-thick chocolate line at least 1 inch down. The vehicles will look as if they are standing on stilts. Set aside to harden.

4. With scissors trim the sides of each cupcake so that it looks like a square from the top. On a flat base arrange the cupcakes, touching one another, in four rows of 5, 4, 5, and 4.

5. Place the fudge icing into a pastry bag with a coupler and a #12 round tip. Pipe the fudge icing so that it covers all of the cupcakes. Once the surface is completely covered, with a metal spatula spread the icing randomly, then carve a shallow indentation for a road.

6. Cover the top of the cupcakes with cookie crumbs, candy, or any other items that will add to the feel of a construction site. Carefully press the vehicles into the cake up to the wheel line. Add any over-piping accents, such as rocks, with the extra chocolate.

7. For fullest flavor, serve the cakes at room temperature.

classic
chocolate cupcakes*

YIELD: 18 CUPCAKES

Here is another must-have for your recipe file. This classic will delight a gaggle of kids or a gathering of your most mature friends. We love them smothered in Matt's Fudge Icing or iced with soft peaks of Kids' Buttercream.

NOTE:

This recipe must be baked in paper cupcake liners, because even if the pan is greased, the batter might stick.

Grease the tops of three 6-mold muffin pans and line them with paper liners. Preheat the oven to 350°F. Have all ingredients at room temperature.

In a saucepan over low heat, melt, whisking often:

- ½ cup milk
- 1 cup brown sugar, packed
- 3 ounces chopped unsweetened chocolate

When chocolate is melted, whisk in:

- 1 large egg yolk

Remove from the heat and set aside.

In the bowl of an electric mixer at medium-high speed, cream:

- 4 ounces (1 stick) unsalted butter

Add and cream until light and fluffy:

- 1 cup granulated sugar

Add slowly, beating well and scraping down after each addition:

- 2 large eggs
- 1 large egg white

On a piece of wax paper, sift together:

- 2 cups cake flour
- 1 teaspoon baking soda
- ½ teaspoon salt

On low speed, add the dry ingredients alternately to the butter and egg mixture with:

- ¾ cup milk
- 1 teaspoon pure vanilla extract

Stir the chocolate mixture into the batter by hand, mixing only until combined.

Pour the batter into the cupcake liners, filling each ⅞ full. Bake for 18 to 20 minutes, or until the tops spring back when lightly pressed.

There is no sting here, but definitely a delicious bite. Our cute and chubby bumblebees take flight from their cupcakes in a blur of yellow nonpareils and edible chocolate wings. Easy to make and fun to eat.

Cake
12 Lemon Poppy Cupcakes (opposite)

Icing
½ recipe of Chocolate Glaze (page 34)

Decoration
2 cups white wafer chocolate and ½ cup dark wafer chocolate to make eyes, stripes, and wings; 1½ cups of yellow nonpareils (online at wilton.com and kitchenkrafts.com)

Colors
blue candy color

Miscellaneous
one 12-mold muffin pan, pastry cones, wing templates (page 173), 1 half-sheet pan, parchment paper or cellophane

HOW TO

1. Bake the cupcakes and let them cool completely. Freeze for 1 hour to overnight.

2. Prepare the glaze.

3. Melt the dark wafer and white wafer chocolates separately. Set aside ⅛ cup of white chocolate for the eyes and highlights. Using the Color Mixing Chart on pages 44–45, tint the remaining white chocolate sky blue. Pour the white, blue, and dark chocolates into separate pastry cones. Keep the chocolates warm on a heating pad or a pan placed over a hot-water bath, since they will be needed in various steps throughout the directions.

4. Using the templates provided, make 12 pairs of wings and 12 stingers. Set aside to harden.

5. Glaze the cupcakes as directed on page 29.

6. Pour the nonpareils into a small bowl. Carefully dip three quarters of the cupcake into the nonpareils; try to create a straight edge where the glaze and nonpareils meet. The glaze will act as the bug's black head.

7. Pipe two white eyes on each head. Pipe chocolate dots on top of the whites to give the effect of googly eyes.

8. At a point ½ inch from the cupcake's edge and perpendicular to the head, press the wings halfway into each cupcake at a 45-degree angle. If necessary, score these points first with a small, sharp knife. Opposite the head, attach the stinger to the cupcake with a dot of chocolate.

9. With the remaining dark chocolate in the pastry cone, pipe 3 to 4 chocolate stripes on the bee's body, parallel to the head's line.

10. For fullest flavor, serve the cakes at room temperature.

lemon poppy cupcakes*

I love desserts that combine textures. One of my favorite accents for any
cake is a thin layer of melted chocolate. Once set, every bite has a crispness to balance the airiness
or moistness of the cake. So I was happy to unite the light lemony flavor with the crunch of poppy
seeds. We enjoy this recipe not just for dessert but as a morning muffin, too.

Grease the top of a 12-mold muffin pan and line it with paper liners. Preheat the oven to 350°F. Have all ingredients at room temperature.

In the bowl of an electric mixer, beat at high speed until light and fluffy:

- 6 ounces (1½ sticks) unsalted butter
- ½ cup granulated sugar
- ¼ cup light brown sugar, packed
- 1 large egg
- ½ teaspoon pure vanilla extract
- 3 tablespoons lemon zest (from 2 lemons)

On a piece of wax paper, sift together:

- 2 cups all-purpose flour
- 1 tablespoon baking powder
- Pinch of salt

At low speed, add the dry ingredients to the butter mixture and mix until just combined.

At low speed, add:

- ½ cup milk
- 2 tablespoons fresh lemon juice
- 1½ tablespoons poppy seeds

Scoop the batter into the prepared molds, filling to the paper liner. Bake for 20 to 25 minutes, or until a cake tester inserted into the center of a cake comes out clean. Cool on a wire rack for 5 to 10 minutes before removing the cupcakes from the pan.

Our creepy spiders and friendly ladybugs come alive in three dimensions. Chocolate legs, fangs, and antennae sprout from their rotund bodies. We glazed the ladybugs in brilliant red but we also make them in green, orange, and yellow at the Bakehouse; apparently, outside of New York, these beetles come in all different colors. As for the spiders, they can be sleek in just chocolate glaze, or add chocolate sprinkles to make a furry arachnid.

We bake both critters in the very versatile bowl pan, which we also use to make sunflowers, eyeballs, jack-o'-lanterns, the planet Earth, floating balloons, or any number of sports balls. See what other designs you can create from it.

In a pinch you can substitute the fudge icing with chilled chocolate glaze to pipe out the spider and ladybug heads.

WHAT YOU WILL NEED:

Cake
12 white chocolate raspberry bowl cakes (see page 124)

Icing
Chocolate Glaze (page 34) for the spiders or White Chocolate Glaze (page 36) for the ladybugs; Matt's Fudge Icing (page 35) (2 cups for spiders, 1½ cups for ladybugs)

Decoration
2 cups dark wafer chocolate and ¼ cup white wafer chocolate to make eyes, smiles, fangs or antennae, legs, and dots; approximately 1½ tablespoons chocolate sprinkles per spider (optional)

Tip
#12 round

Colors
green and yellow candy color for the spider and red liquid gel color for the ladybug

Miscellaneous
two mini bowl pans; pastry cones; leg, antennae, eye, smile, and fang templates (page 169); 1 half-sheet pan; parchment paper or cellophane; wire rack for glazing; twelve 6-inch (or larger) bases

1. Bake the cakes and let them cool completely. Freeze for 1 hour to overnight.

2. Prepare the glaze of your choice. If making the ladybugs, tint the white chocolate glaze red with liquid gel, paste, or liquid colors.

3. Melt the dark wafer and white wafer chocolates separately. If making the spiders, set aside ⅛ cup of the white chocolate. Using the Color Mixing Chart on pages 44—45, tint the remaining white chocolate neon green.

4. Using the templates provided, make 12 sets of legs and 12 spider fangs, or 12 sets of ladybug antennae, dots, eyes, and smiles as illustrated in The Chocolate Method (pages 40—43). Set aside to harden.

5. Glaze the cakes as directed on page 29. You may have to glaze the ladybugs twice— in which case, freeze the cakes in between coats for best results. If desired, make the spiders hairy by encrusting them with chocolate sprinkles before plating.

6. With an offset metal spatula, carefully place each cake onto its serving plate or base.

7. Place the fudge icing into a pastry bag with a coupler, and with a #12 tip pipe a 1-inch-diameter dot in the front of each cake for the critter's head. For spiders, pipe four ½-inch dots on each side of the body starting at least ½ inch from the head.

8. For the spiders, press the fangs into the base of the head. Pipe eight neon green eyes on each head. Pipe chocolate dots on top of each eye to give the effect of googly eyes. For the ladybugs, stick the eyes and smile to the fudge head.

9. For the spider, press the legs into the small fudge dots and if possible a little into the edge of the cake for stability, resting the bottom edge of the legs on the base. For the ladybug, press the legs into the abdomen, about ½ inch up from the base, resting the feet on the base.

10. For the ladybug, pour 1 tablespoon of melted chocolate into a pastry cone. Cut a medium-size hole and pipe a line running from the base of the head to the back of the abdomen. Place 3 chocolate dots on each side of this line.

11. For fullest flavor, serve the cakes at room temperature.

white chocolate raspberry cakes*

YIELD: 12 MINI BOWLS

While writing our Christmas cookie book, we developed a recipe for our spritz machine that used raspberry extract. We liked the flavor so much we decided to add it to our white chocolate cake; after all, raspberry and chocolate are a match made in heaven, and it's no different with white chocolate.

Grease two 6-mold mini bowl pans. Preheat the oven to 350°F. Have all ingredients at room temperature.

In a double boiler or in a medium metal bowl placed over a hot-water bath, melt:
- 4½ ounces chopped white chocolate

If not at body temperature, set aside and let cool to body temperature.

In the bowl of an electric mixer, beat at high speed until light and fluffy:
- 6 ounces (1½ sticks) unsalted butter
- ¾ cup sugar

Add the melted chocolate and mix until combined.

On a piece of wax paper, sift together:
- 2¼ cups cake flour
- 1 tablespoon baking powder
- ¼ teaspoon salt

Add the dry ingredients to the butter mixture alternately with:
- ¾ cup milk
- ¾ teaspoon pure vanilla extract
- 1½ teaspoons raspberry extract

In a separate small bowl, beat until foamy:
- 3 large egg whites

Continue beating the whites at high speed while gradually adding:
- 2¼ tablespoons sugar

When stiff (but not dry) peaks form, fold the whites into the cake batter with a rubber spatula. Blend just until the whites are evenly distributed.

Pour the batter into the prepared molds. Bake for 20 to 25 minutes, or until a cake tester inserted into the center of a cake comes out clean. Cool the cakes on a wire rack for 15 to 20 minutes before turning them out of their pans.

shark cakes**

Years ago, one of our former cake decorators, Rob Berner, made a batch of these shark cakes for the storefront. I loved them immediately because they are goofy, morbid, and fun all at once, and I have been making them ever since. To make them even more gory, I used a Red Velvet cake filled with Chopped Cherry Whipped Cream. What was this shark's last meal?

WHAT YOU WILL NEED:

Cake
8 Red Velvet cone cakes (see page 127)

Icing
one and a quarter recipes of Kaye's Buttercream (page 32) or one recipe House Buttercream (page 31)

Filling
Chopped Cherry Whipped Cream (page 127)

Decoration
¼ cup dark wafer chocolate and 1½ cups white wafer chocolate to make eyes and fins

Colors
red, royal blue, teal, and (optional) orange liquid gel colors, and blue candy color

Miscellaneous
two mini cone pans, pastry bag, coupler, pastry cones, eye and fin templates (page 170), 1 half-sheet pan, parchment paper or cellophane, turntable, eight 6-inch (or larger) bases

1. Bake the cakes and let them cool completely. Prepare the buttercream.

2. Prepare the filling. To fill the cake, cut each cone in half horizontally and, with a small paring knife, cut out a 2-inch-long x ¾-inch-deep cone from the bottom of the cake and a 1-inch-long x ¾-inch-deep cone from the top. Fill the holes with a generous amount of Chopped Cherry Whipped Cream and replace the top on the cone. Scrape off any Chopped Cherry Whipped Cream that may have come through the seam. Chill for 30 minutes.

3. Melt the dark wafer and white wafer chocolates separately. Set aside ⅛ cup white chocolate for the eyes. Using the Color Mixing Chart on pages 44—45, tint the remaining white chocolate royal blue. Using the templates provided, make 8 sets of tail fins, 8 dorsal fins, and 8 pairs of eyes as illustrated in The Chocolate Method (pages 40—43). Set aside to harden.

4. Set aside 1¼ cups of uncolored buttercream. Prepare the colored buttercream: approximately 2 cups royal blue, ⅛ cup red, 1 cup teal, and (optional) 2 tablespoons pale peach.

5. Remove the cakes from the refrigerator. Place a cake in the center of a turntable. Cover the shark four fifths with blue and one fifth with white. Make sure there is extra buttercream at the top of the cake to create the point of the shark's head. Finish icing the cone as directed in Smooth Icing on a Shaped Cake (page 28) with one exception: pull the cellophane up from the base, but do not curve it over the top of the dome; instead just continue pulling up at the same angle. Continue around the cake in the same manner until a point forms.

6. Using an offset spatula, carefully place the cake onto its base.

7. With a small offset spatula, spread the teal buttercream around the base of the shark, pulling some up onto the shark's head. Spread some white buttercream randomly on top, pulling the spatula straight up to create the look of white caps.

8. Place the remaining red buttercream into a pastry cone and cut a medium hole in the tip. Free-hand pipe the mouth.

9. Place the remaining white buttercream into a pastry cone and cut a small to medium hole in the tip. To pipe teeth on the edge of the mouth, squeeze while holding the tip in place until you have the size base you desire, then pull down or up (depending on whether you are piping the upper or lower teeth) as you release the pressure, ending with a sharp point.

10. Press the wide-set eyes into the shark's head above the mouth. Pipe two nostrils at the top of the head with chocolate.

11. Press the back fin into the shark's back near the base and the dorsal fins at its side. With an offset spatula, gently carve gills on both sides of the shark above the fins.

12. If you wish, place the pale peach buttercream into a pastry cone with a medium tip. For those with a love of the grotesque, free-hand pipe a human body in the water, using the photograph on page 28 as a guide. Repeat with the remaining 7 cones.

13. For fullest flavor, serve the cakes at room temperature.

red velvet*

YIELD: 8 CONES OR 18 CUPCAKES

Red velvet cake is all the rage these days, and I understand why. Its nostalgic look and simple flavors appeal to just about anyone. During the holidays we like to mix it up a little and make red and blue velvet for the Fourth of July or orange and green velvet for St. Patty's Day.

If you are making Shark Cakes, grease two mini (4-mold) cone pans.

If you are making cupcakes, grease the top of three 6-mold muffin pans and line them with paper liners. Preheat the oven to 350°F. Have all ingredients at room temperature.

In the bowl of an electric mixer, beat at high speed until light and fluffy:

- 8 ounces (2 sticks) unsalted butter
- 1½ cups sugar

Add and beat on medium speed until well creamed:

- 2 large eggs
- 1 tablespoon red liquid gel color or 3 tablespoons McCormick's red food-coloring

On a piece of wax paper, sift together:

- 2½ cups cake flour
- 2 tablespoons cocoa powder
- 1 teaspoon baking soda
- 1 teaspoon salt

At low speed, add the dry ingredients to the butter mixture alternately with:

- 1 cup buttermilk
- 1 teaspoon pure vanilla extract
- 1 teaspoon vinegar

Pour the batter into the prepared molds, filling each three-quarters full. Bake for 20 to 25 minutes, or until a cake tester inserted into the center of a cake comes out clean. Cool on a wire rack for 10 to 15 minutes before turning the cone-shaped cakes out of the pans or removing the cupcakes from the pans.

CHOPPED CHERRY WHIPPED CREAM*

YIELD: 3 CUPS

In the bowl of an electric mixer fitted with a whisk attachment, whip until stiff:

- 1⅓ cups heavy cream
- ¼ cup confectioners' sugar
- 1 teaspoon pure vanilla extract

Fold in:

- ¾ cup chopped cherries (fresh, frozen, or canned) with up to 3 tablespoons of their juice

a day at the beach***

To celebrate the start of summer, to throw a festive beach party, or to say to the hot weather when Labor Day rolls around, these little beach pails will have you wanting to run down to the water's edge to build one more sand castle. To echo the sandy colors, we filled our pails with caramel cake and dulce de leche buttercream. To complete the scene, chocolate shovels, shells, and starfish float along the shore.

This design is one of the more time-consuming in the book. To save time, limit the palette: instead of mixing all of the colors, just choose two or three.

WHAT YOU WILL NEED:

Cake
four 4-inch round Caramel Cakes to make three beach pails (page 79)

Icing
Kaye's Buttercream (page 32) or House Buttercream (page 31), Dulce de Leche (page 101)

Decoration
¼ cup dark wafer chocolate and 3 cups white wafer chocolate to make 3 chocolate shovels,

3 handles, 3 starfish, 3 clam shells, 3 sand dollars, 3 mussels, and 3 oyster shells; 1 cup ground nuts, ground butter cookies, cake crumbs, or graham cracker crumbs for sand; ¼ cup clear edible gel for water.

Colors
red and teal liquid gel colors, and yellow, orange, blue, purple, and pink candy colors

Tips
#89 triple-line tip, #81 mum tip (as small as #79 can be substituted)

Miscellaneous
four 4-inch round cake pans; three 4-inch thin cardboard rounds, or three thick grease-proof paper rounds; one 3⅛-round cardboard or thick paper template; pastry bag; coupler; pastry cones; shell, shovel, and handle templates (page 170); 1 half-sheet pan, parchment paper or cellophane, turntable, four 8-inch (or larger) bases

1. Bake the cakes and let cool. Prepare the Dulce de Leche and the buttercream. Set aside ¼ cup uncolored buttercream. Prepare the colored and flavored buttercream: 1 cup red, about 2½ cups of Dulce de Leche Buttercream (page 33).

2. Trim the domes off of each cake and set aside in an airtight container. Cut each cake into three layers. Stack 4 layers per cake onto three 4-inch cardboard rounds. Fill the cakes with the Dulce de Leche Buttercream as directed in Filling a Cake (page 23). Chill for at least 30 minutes to overnight.

3. Melt the dark wafer and white wafer chocolates separately. Set aside ½ cup white. Using the Color Mixing Chart on pages 44—45, tint the remaining white chocolate: about ½ cup royal blue, 2 tablespoons pale orange, 2 tablespoons coral, 2 tablespoons yellow, 1 tablespoon light brown, 1 tablespoon violet. Using the templates provided, make 3 of each: shovels, handles, starfish, sand dollars, oyster shells, mussels, and clam shells as illustrated in The Chocolate Method (pages 40—43). Set aside to harden.

4. Remove the cakes from the refrigerator. Place the 3⅛-inch round template in the center of the cake. Using the top template and the bottom cardboard round as a guide, with a serrated knife, carve the cake at an angle around the entire circumference of the cake until you have an upside-down pail shape. Make sure the cakes are level, because what is now the top will become the bottom. Crumb-coat the cakes with Dulce de Leche Buttercream as directed (page 24). Chill for at least 30 minutes.

5. Ice the beach pails with red buttercream as directed in Smooth Icing on a Cake (page 27). The tops should have only a scraping of buttercream.

6. Place the remaining red buttercream in a pastry bag with a coupler, and with a #89 tip pipe a strip of lines around the center of each pail.

7. To invert your cakes, hold one cake at a time on its round in your hand and carefully place a covered cardboard round or base onto the top of the cake. Steady the base with one hand and the cake with the other hand and invert. The beach pail should now be right side up. Repeat with the remaining cakes.

8. Remove the cardboard rounds from the top of each cake. Place a dollop of Dulce Buttercream on top of each cake and place the reserved domes on top. Spread more Dulce Buttercream over the top of each cake, then sprinkle with your "sand" material.

9. Change the tip of the red pastry bag to #81 and, with the concave side of the tip overlapping the top edge of the cake, pipe the top rim of the beach pail.

10. Carefully drape the handle over the pail, resting it over the rim and on the side.

11. Mix 1 drop of teal liquid-gel color with the clear piping gel. Spread onto one half of the base. If desired, spread Dulce Buttercream over the other half of the base and sprinkle with nuts and/or crumbs.

12. Place the shells and the shovel around the base of the pail.

13. For fullest flavor, serve the cakes at room temperature.

flower power*

Flowers are just one way to make a rather whimsical treat like the cupcake into a pretty and elegant dessert. I've made the tops of these cupcakes look like roses, chrysanthemums, sunflowers, hydrangeas, peonies, poppies, and Gerbera daisies. Many of the petals are variegated to give them a natural appearance. This is achieved by spreading a thin strip of either a lighter or darker shade of buttercream up one side of a pastry bag, then filling the rest of the bag with the main color. Use the Color Mixing Chart on pages 44—45 to help you mix the colors you want.

By tiering the cupcakes, either on stacked cake pedestals or in a pastry tree (a wire structure used for displaying pastries or cupcakes, available at some baking supply stores and Wilton), you can further enhance the feeling of elegance—perfect for that special day, since more than ever brides and grooms are opting for cupcakes instead of the traditional tiered cake.

For best results, make certain your buttercream has a medium consistency so the petals will hold their shape. Piped flowers, as in nature, are unique and irregular. Don't be intimidated by the piping process; just let the petals flow from the pastry bag. Take a step back from your creation and I am sure you will see how all of the petals fuse into a beautiful flower.

WHAT YOU WILL NEED:

Cake
12 Lemon Coconut Cupcakes (page 136)

Icing
Kaye's Buttercream (page 32) or House Buttercream (page 31). You will need between 2¾ and 5 cups of buttercream depending on the flowers you are making.

Decoration
½ to 1 cup dark wafer chocolate (only needed for some types of flowers)

Colors
See individual flower directions for colors (below).

Tips
Tips are noted in individual flower directions (below).

Miscellaneous
one 12-mold muffin pan, pastry bag, coupler, pastry cones, turntable

1. Bake the cupcakes and let them cool completely. Freeze for 1 hour to overnight.

2. Prepare the icing. Tint the icing according to the individual flower recipe.

3. Follow the directions below for piping out flowers.

4. For fullest flavor, serve the cakes at room temperature.

rose

(SEE VARIATIONS BELOW)

To cover 12 cupcakes you will need 4½ cups buttercream: 1½ cups white and 3 cups pale pink.

Colors: Red or neon pink liquid gel colors

Tip: #104 petal tip (you can substitute #103)

1. Place a coupler into a pastry bag. Using a small metal spatula, spread a strip of white buttercream up one side of the bag's interior. Fill the rest of the bag with pale pink. Try to line up the narrow end of the petal tip with the white strip.

2. Place the cupcake on the center of a turntable.

3. For the first row of petals, spin the turntable clockwise. With the narrow end of the tip running along the outer edge of the cupcake, pipe 6 long petals around the circumference of the cupcake. Allow the tip to stay flush with the cupcake, most likely angled downward with the slope of the dome.

4. Continue spinning the turntable clockwise and pipe a second row of 6 to 8 petals inside the first. The wide end of the tip should touch the previous row of petals. Flare the end of the tip upward from the previous row, approximately 30 degrees.

5. Holding the tip at a 45-degree angle, pipe 6 petals for the third row.

6. For the fourth row of petals, spin the turntable counterclockwise and pipe five almost vertical petals. Pipe 4 to 5 vertical petals for the fifth row. Angle the tip inward approximately 10 degrees and pipe 3 petals for the sixth row.

7. The last row is one petal. To make the petal flare, pull the tip upward slightly, squeezing a little more at the center, and then pull the tip back down toward the starting point and tail off. The petal will resemble a bud.

Variations: To make a ranunculus, pipe an additional 3 rows of petals. Keep the rows and petals tight together.

To make a peony, follow the directions for the rose but apply inconsistent pressure and slightly shake the tip while piping each petal. This will create a ruffled effect.

each petal. To finish each petal, drag the tip toward the center as you release the pressure. The wide end of the tip should remain close to the center. Begin the next petal so that it slightly overlaps the first. Repeat for each blossom.

4   Place the yellow buttercream into a pastry cone and cut a small hole in its tip. Pipe a yellow dot in the center of each blossom.

gerbera daisy

To cover 12 cupcakes you will need approximately 4 cups buttercream: ½ cup white, 3¼ cups periwinkle, and 2 tablespoons yellow.

Colors: Blue, violet, and yellow liquid gel colors

Tip: # 102 petal tip (you can substitute # 103)

1   Place a coupler into a pastry bag. Using a small metal spatula, spread a strip of white buttercream up one side of the bag's interior. Fill the rest of the bag with periwinkle. Try to line up the narrow end of the petal tip with the white strip.

2   Place the cupcake on the center of a turntable.

3   Most blossoms have 5 evenly spaced petals of equal size, but the hydrangea has 4 petals. Pipe small four-petal blossoms as follows, covering the entire cupcake. Choose a center point for the flower. Place the wide end of the tip at the center point. Place the narrow end of the tip at a 30-degree angle to the cake surface. Pivoting the tip around the center point, pipe the first petal by increasing pressure as you move the tip around. The curvature of the petal occurs not from moving the tip up and back toward the center point, but from increasing the pressure toward the middle of

To cover 12 cupcakes you will need 3¼ cups buttercream: 2¼ cups hot pink and ¾ cup bright purple, 2 tablespoons orange, 2 tablespoons yellow.

Colors: Neon pink, violet, yellow, and orange liquid gel colors

Chocolate: ¾ cup dark wafer chocolate

Tip: #104 petal tip (you can substitute #103)

1   Place a coupler into a pastry bag. Using a small metal spatula, spread a strip of bright purple buttercream up one side of the bag's interior. Fill the rest of the bag with hot pink. Try to line up the narrow end of the petal tip with the bright purple strip.

2. Place the cupcake on the center of a turntable.

3. Hold the bag perpendicular to the cupcake. Starting at the outer edge of the cupcake, and the outer edge of each petal, squeeze and move the tip inward. Release the pressure as you move in toward the center point.

4. Fill the cupcake with more petals in the same way, fanning out in a circle from the center point. Overlap the first row of petals with smaller petals to disguise the cupcake's surface.

5. Melt the dark wafer chocolate and pour it into a pastry cone. Cut a medium hole in its tip and fill in the center of the flower.

6. Place the yellow and orange buttercreams into pastry cones. Cut small holes in the tips and pipe yellow and orange dots within the chocolate center.

poppy

To cover 12 cupcakes you will need 3 ⅛ cups buttercream: 3 cups red and ⅛ cup yellow.

Colors: Red and yellow liquid gel colors

Chocolate: ¾ cup dark wafer chocolate

Tip: #104 petal tip (you can substitute #103)

1. Place the red buttercream into a pastry bag with a coupler and a petal tip.

2. Place the cupcake on the center of a turntable.

3. Spin the turntable while piping each row of petals. With the narrow end of the tip running along the outer edge of the cupcake, pipe 5 petals around the circumference of the cupcake. Allow the tip to stay flush with the cupcake, most likely angled downward with the slope of the dome. Apply inconsistent pressure and slightly shake the tip while piping each petal. This will create a ruffled effect.

4. Continue spinning the turntable and pipe a second row of 8 petals. The wide end of the tip should touch the previous row of petals. Flare the end of the tip upward from the previous row, approximately 30 degrees. Continue to apply inconsistent pressure and shake the tip.

5. With the tip at a 45-degree angle, pipe 6 petals for the last row.

6. Remove the petal tip and pipe a large red dot in the center of the flower to equalize the height of the cupcake with the petals.

7. Melt the dark wafer chocolate and pour it into a pastry cone. Cut a medium hole in its tip and fill in the center of the flower.

8. Place the yellow buttercream into a pastry cone. Cut a small hole in the tip and pipe yellow dots within the chocolate center.

sunflower

To cover 12 cupcakes you will need 2¼ cups buttercream: 1½ cups yellow and ¾ cup orange.

Colors: Yellow and orange liquid gel colors

Chocolate: 1½ cups dark wafer chocolate

Tip: #352 leaf tip (you can substitute #67)

1. Place a coupler in a pastry bag. Using a small metal spatula, spread a strip of orange buttercream up one side of the bag's interior. Fill the rest of the bag with yellow.

2. Fill a pastry cone with some of the variegated buttercream from the pastry bag. Set aside.

3. Place the cupcake on the center of a turntable.

4. For the first petal row start ¾ inch from the edge of the cupcake, hold the pastry bag at a 30-degree angle and squeeze, then release the pressure as you move away from the center.

5. Overlap this row of petals with another row, between the petals of the first row. Hold the bag at a 45-degree angle.

6. Melt the dark wafer chocolate and pour it into a pastry cone. Cut a medium hole in its tip and fill in the center of the flower.

7. Cut a small hole in the tip of the pastry cone containing the variegated buttercream and pipe small seeds within the chocolate center.

dahlia

To cover 12 cupcakes you will need 3 cups buttercream: 2¼ cups bright purple and ¾ cup pale violet.

Colors: Neon pink and violet liquid gel colors

Tip: #79 tip (you can substitute #80 or #81)

1. Place a coupler in a pastry bag. Using a small metal spatula, spread a strip of bright purple buttercream up one side of the bag's interior. Fill the rest of the bag with violet.

2. Place the cupcake on the center of a turntable.

3. Holding the convex end of the pastry tip down, pipe a row of petals around the outer edge. Start each petal ½ inch from the edge and pull away from the center. For this first row allow the tip to stay flush with the cupcake, angled downward with the slope of the dome. Each petal should be ½ to ¾ inch long.

4. Pipe another row inside the first, overlapping the petals of the first row about halfway. Increase the angle of the petals by approximately 15 to 20 degrees per row. Finish by filling in the center with petals. The petals in the center will be almost vertical.

lemon coconut cupcakes*

YIELD: 12 CUPCAKES

Since coconut is wonderful whether it is paired with chocolate, custard, lemon, or lime, we made a light and tangy variation of our Chocolate Coconut Cupcakes that is perfect for a spring celebration or a June wedding. An old-fashioned Kids' Buttercream is all you need to top them off, or make blooming flowers with piped buttercream (see page 131).

Grease the top of a 12-mold muffin pan and line it with paper liners. Preheat the oven to 350°F. Have all ingredients at room temperature.

In the bowl of an electric mixer, beat at high speed until light and fluffy:
- 6 ounces (1½ sticks) unsalted butter
- 1 cup sugar

Add one at a time and beat on medium speed until well creamed:
- 3 large eggs

Add and mix to combine:
- 2 tablespoons lemon zest
- 1½ teaspoons pure vanilla extract

On a piece of wax paper, sift together:
- 1½ cups all-purpose flour
- ¼ teaspoon baking soda
- ¼ teaspoon salt

At low speed, add the dry ingredients to the butter mixture alternately with:
- ¼ cup buttermilk

Add and mix until combined:
- ¼ cup fresh lemon juice

Fold in:
- 1 cup toasted sweetened coconut

Scoop the batter into the prepared molds, filling each to the top of the paper liner. Bake for 20 to 25 minutes, or until a cake tester inserted into the center of a cupcake comes out clean. The tops should spring back when lightly touched. Cool on a wire rack for 5 to 10 minutes before removing the cupcakes from their pan.

. . . . *Unless it is a cake.* Yet again I was inspired by a pan I found in a Williams-Sonoma store. I wanted to make something unique and was quite excited by my prospects. Unfortunately, my first plan failed. I had wanted to cover the roses with tinted White Chocolate Glaze, but the glaze settled into the crevices between the petals, leaving me with a lovely red blob. Because our Almond Cake is so moist, I decided to leave the rose cakes unglazed, but I did tint the batter pink. I then arranged the baked cakes in a bouquet and made chocolate leaves and stems to tie them all together. Instead of serving the cakes in a bouquet, a simpler alternative is to plate each rose individually with two chocolate leaves.

Cake
12 mini rose Almond Cakes to make 1 bouquet (opposite)

Icing
½ recipe Chocolate Glaze (optional, page 34), ¼ cup buttercream (optional; storebought or House [page 31], Kaye's [page 32], or Kids' [page 33])

Decoration
1 cup white wafer chocolate to make leaves and stems, buttercream bow (optional)

Colors
green candy color, pink liquid gel color (optional)

Tip
#104 petal tip (you can substitute #103)

Miscellaneous
one mini rose pan, pastry cones, leaf templates (page 173), 1 half-sheet pan, parchment paper or cellophane, 14-inch or larger base

HOW TO

1 Bake the cakes and let them cool completely.

2 Melt the white wafer chocolate. Using the Color Mixing Chart (pages 44–45), tint the white chocolate: approximately ¼ cup light green and ¼ cup dark green. In a small glass or plastic bowl, set aside approximately 1 tablespoon of the dark green chocolate. Using the templates provided, make 12 small and 12 large leaves. Set aside to harden.

3 Arrange the roses in a cluster of 4 rows offset from the center of the base: 2 roses on top, followed by rows of 3, 4, and 3 below it (refer to the photograph).

4 Remelt the reserved dark green chocolate and pour it into a pastry cone. Cut a small hole at the tip and pipe stems from the bottom of the cluster to the edge of the base.

5 Nestle the leaves into and around the bouquet and stems.

6 Optional: Tint the buttercream pink and place it into a pastry bag with a coupler and a #104 petal tip. First pipe a ribbon around the stems, then pipe a bow: Hold the bag at a 45-degree angle to the surface. With the wide end of the tip pointed down, squeeze, moving the tip up and around to the right, ending at the starting point. Then, starting at the same point, squeeze, moving the tip up and around to the left, again ending at the starting point. At the starting point, squeeze two ribbons down to finish off the bow.

7 For fullest flavor, serve the cakes at room temperature.

almond cakes*

A customer from North Carolina sent us this recipe and requested we make it for her when she was in town. Reminiscent of marzipan, this moist cake was so delicious we're sharing it with you. At the Bakehouse we also bake the Almond Cake in a sheet pan and make it into petits fours.

Grease well and flour one 12-mold mini rose pan. Preheat the oven to 350°F. Have all ingredients at room temperature.

In the bowl of an electric mixer, beat at medium speed until crumbly:

- ¾ cup sugar
- 8 ounces almond paste

Add and mix until light and fluffy:

- 4 ounces (1 stick) unsalted butter

Add one at a time and beat on medium speed until well creamed:

- 3 large eggs

Add and mix to combine:

- 1½ teaspoons rum
- ½ teaspoon almond extract
- 5 drops pink food coloring, or tint to your liking (optional)

Mix together and add to the butter mixture at low speed just until combined:

- ¼ cup all-purpose flour
- ⅓ teaspoon baking powder
- ¼ teaspoon salt

Do not over-mix.

Scoop the batter into the prepared molds, filling each mold three-quarters full. Bake for 20 to 25 minutes, or until golden. The tops should spring back when lightly pressed. Immediately remove the cakes from their pan by placing a parchment-lined sheet pan on top of the baked cakes and inverting. Carefully remove.

basket cupcakes**

Our carrot cupcakes are transformed into a woven basket, complete with an edible chocolate handle and a spattering of spring blossoms. Fill this treat with piped eggs or jelly beans and you have yourself an Easter basket. We also like to make these dainty baskets for baby showers because they are so cute, just like the little bundle of joy that is on the way.

WHAT YOU WILL NEED:

Cake
18 Carrot Cupcakes (page 143)

Icing
1½ recipes Kaye's Buttercream (page 32), 12 ounces semisweet chocolate to make chocolate buttercream

Decoration
2 cups white wafer chocolate and ⅛ cup dark wafer chocolate to make 20 handles

Colors
Violet, green, and yellow liquid gel colors and orange candy color (optional)

Tips
#6, 7, or 8 round tip; #101, 102, or 103 petal tip; # 263 small leaf tip

Miscellaneous
three 6-mold muffin pans, pastry bag, coupler, pastry cones, handle template (page 170), 1 half-sheet pan, parchment paper or cellophane, turntable

1. Bake the cupcakes and let them cool completely. Freeze for 1 hour to overnight.

2. Prepare the buttercream.

3. Prepare the colored and flavored buttercream: approximately 4 cups chocolate buttercream, 1½ generous cups of violet, ½ generous cup of green, and 2 tablespoons yellow.

4. Melt the dark wafer and white wafer chocolates together. Add 4 drops of orange candy color to enhance the color. Using the template provided, make eighteen handles, as illustrated in The Chocolate Method (pages 40—43). Set aside to harden.

5. When the chocolate has set, using the same chocolate bag, over-pipe a scalloped edge or rickrack (zigzag) pattern to simulate the braiding of a real basket handle. Set aside to harden. When set, gently flip the handle and pipe the same pattern on the opposite side.

6. Ice the cupcakes with a smooth finish as directed on page 26. The icing on the outer edge of the cupcake should rise at least ½ inch from the paper's edge.

7. Place the chocolate buttercream into a pastry bag with a coupler, and with a round tip pipe a 2 x 2-inch basket weave (see below) around the edge of each cupcake. Placing the cupcake on a turntable will make this easier. Don't go below the paper line.

8. Mark where the handle will go by gently pressing it into the buttercream. If the cupcake is still frozen, use a knife or other small, sharp object to puncture the cupcake in these two spots. This will make it easier to push the handle into the cake later.

9. Place the violet buttercream into a pastry bag with a coupler, and with a petal tip pipe a blossom (see Hydrangea, page 133) in the center of the cupcake. Then pipe approximately 6 more blossoms around it, avoiding the holes made for the handle.

10. Place the yellow buttercream into a pastry cone and cut a small hole in the tip. Pipe yellow dots in the center of each flower.

11. Place the green buttercream into a pastry bag with a coupler, and with a leaf tip pipe leaves sporadically among the blossoms.

12. Stick the chocolate handle into the holes, pressing it halfway into the cupcake.

13. For fullest flavor, serve the cakes at room temperature.

BASKET WEAVE

Holding the bag perpendicular to the cake surface, pipe a vertical line where you want to begin the basket weave. Holding the bag at a 45-degree angle to the cake, pipe equidistant horizontal lines, separated by the width of the tip, overlapping the vertical line by ⅓ inch on each side. Approximately ⅛ inch to the right of the first vertical line, and slightly overlapping the horizontal lines, pipe another vertical line. Pipe another set of horizontal lines, starting in the empty spaces formed between the first set of horizontal lines, overlapping the second vertical line by ½ inch. Continue this pattern.

carrot cupcakes*

YIELD: 18 CUPCAKES

Back in 1988, when my mom opened her first bakery, the Runcible Spoon in Nyack, New York, she offered ten different muffins. This recipe is one of the originals: yet *another muffin that is transformed into a delicious cupcake. Bake them for breakfast, ice them* with Kids' Buttercream, or make them into adorable little baskets (see page 141).

Grease the tops of three 6-mold muffin pans and line them with paper liners. Preheat the oven to 350°F. Have all ingredients at room temperature.

In a large bowl, mix well:
- 2 cups sugar
- 1¼ cups vegetable oil
- 4 large eggs

On a piece of wax paper, sift together:
- 2½ cups all-purpose flour
- 1 teaspoon baking powder
- 1½ teaspoons baking soda
- 1 teaspoon salt
- 1 tablespoon ground cinnamon
- 1 tablespoon ground ginger

Add the dry ingredients to the wet ingredients and mix to combine.

Add just to combine:
- 1 cup chopped walnuts
- ¾ cup raisins
- 3 cups grated carrots (about 1 pound of carrots)

Scoop the batter into the prepared molds, filling each to the top of the paper liner. Bake for 20 to 25 minutes, or until a cake tester inserted into the center of a cake comes out clean. Cool on a wire rack for 5 to 10 minutes before removing the cupcakes from their pans.

gâteau chapeau***

Before I ever made my first edible hat, I had a name for it: Gâteau Chapeau. Mother's Day was the first holiday to showcase a 3-D bonnet. Since then we have added baseball caps for Father's Day, and witch hats for Halloween. In addition to these Bakehouse favorites, I added a fedora with a feather tucked in its band, perfect for a cool cat.

witch hats

WHAT YOU WILL NEED:

Cake: To make 4 hats, bake 2 scant 6-inch rounds and 4 mini cones of Pecan Cake (page 149)

Icing: $1/2$ recipe Whipped Chocolate Ganache (page 105), Chocolate Glaze (page 34), $1/4$ recipe Kids' Buttercream for ribbon (optional; page 33)

Decoration: $1/2$ cup white wafer chocolate to make 4 witch buckles, Chocolate Plastic for ribbons (optional; page 109)

Tip: #45 flat tip (you can substitute a #104 petal tip)

Colors: violet liquid gel color and orange and yellow candy colors

Miscellaneous: two 6-inch round pans and one 4-mold mini cone pan, pastry bag, coupler, pastry cones, buckle template (page 170), 1 half-sheet pan, parchment paper or cellophane, turntable, wire rack for glazing, four 6-inch cardboard rounds, four 8-inch (or larger) bases

HOW TO

1 Bake the cakes and let them cool completely. If opting for Chocolate Plastic rib-
bons, prepare the Chocolate Plastic. If opting for a buttercream ribbon, prepare the Kids' Buttercream. Prepare the Whipped Chocolate Ganache and Chocolate Glaze.

2 To set up the cakes: Cut the 6-inch round cakes horizontally into 2 equal layers. Cut the bottom dome off of the cones. Place each 6-inch layer onto a 6-inch cardboard or thick grease-proof paper round.

3 Crumb-coat the 6-inch rounds with a thin layer of Whipped Chocolate Ganache. Place the remaining ganache into a pastry bag with a coupler and pipe a large point on the top of the cone. With a piece of cellophane, smooth out the ganache where it meets the cake to make a flush connection. Freeze for 1 hour.

4 Melt the white wafer chocolate. Using the Color Mixing Chart on pages 44—45, tint the white chocolate: approximately 1 tablespoon yellow and 1 tablespoon orange. Using the template provided, make 4 buckles as illustrated in The Chocolate Method (pages 40—43). Set aside to harden.

5 Glaze the tops and bottoms of the cakes with Chocolate Glaze as directed in Chocolate Glaze on Cake, pages 29—30. If possible, invert and submerge the tip of each hat into the glaze before glazing as usual. This will ensure that the tip gets covered.

6 Place the bottom of the hat on its base. With the help of a metal spatula, carefully place the cone in the center of the base.

7 Buttercream Ribbon (see Note): Prepare $1/4$ cup violet buttercream. Place the violet buttercream into a pastry bag with a coupler, and with a #45 flat tip pipe a flat ribbon border (see page 163) around the base of the cone. Chocolate Plastic Ribbon: Tint half of the plastic violet. Dust a clean, flat surface with cornstarch. With a rolling pin, roll out the plastic to $1/8$ inch thick. Cut it

into four ¾ x 10-inch strips. Place one end of the strip down on the cake starting at the base of the hat, carefully draping around until it meets itself. Using scissors, cut off any extra plastic.

8   Place the buckle on the ribbon. Pipe 3 chocolate dots (buckle holes) to the right of the buckle.

9   For fullest flavor, serve the cakes at room temperature.

NOTE:

If you are only making witch hats and you don't have buttercream on hand, you can buy a package of vanilla icing at the store and tint it violet.

straw hats

WHAT YOU WILL NEED:

Cake: To make 6 hats, bake 3 scant 6-inch rounds and 6 mini bowls of Pecan Cake (page 149)

Icing: Kaye's Buttercream (page 32)

Tips: #6 or 7 round tip, #103 or 104 petal tip

Colors: yellow, brown, pink, and green liquid gel colors

Miscellaneous: three 6-inch round pans, one 6-mold mini bowl pan, pastry bag, coupler, pastry cones, turntable, six 8-inch (or larger) bases

HOW TO

1   Bake the cakes and let them cool completely. Prepare the buttercream.

2   Cut the 6-inch round cakes horizontally into 2 equal layers. Cut the bottom dome off of the bowls. Place each 6-inch round cake, crumb side down, onto a 6-inch cardboard or thick grease-proof paper round, adhering it with a dollop of buttercream. Place a bowl in the center of each 6-inch round cake, again adhering with a dollop of buttercream. Adhere the cardboard round supporting the cakes to their bases.

3   Set aside ¼ cup uncolored buttercream. Prepare the colored buttercream: approximately 6 cups straw-yellow, ¼ cup pink, 2 tablespoons green, 1 tablespoon yellow.

4   Place the straw-yellow buttercream into a pastry bag with a coupler, and with a #6 round tip pipe a basket-weave pattern. Start with the brim of the hat: pipe the vertical lines so that they are closer together near the top edge and wider apart at the base, like the sun's rays. In a similar manner pipe basket weave on the hat's bowl-top. All of the vertical lines should meet at the apex of the hat. The horizontal lines will be shorter and thinner the closer they approach the top of the dome.

5   Place the pink buttercream into a pastry bag with a #103 petal tip. Pipe a flat ribbon border around the bowl base. Pipe a bow in the front by holding the bag at a 45-degree angle to the cake surface. With the wide end of the tip pointed down, squeeze, moving the tip up and around to the right, end-

ing at the starting point. Then, starting at the same point, squeeze, moving the tip up and around to the left again, ending at the starting point. At the starting point squeeze two ribbons down to finish off the bow.

6. Place the pink, green, and yellow buttercream into separate pastry cones. Cut small holes in the tips of the each. Pipe out green stems and leaves onto the hat. Pipe white daisies on the tops of the stems (see photograph). Pipe yellow dots in the center of each flower. See the photograph for reference.

7. For fullest flavor, serve the cakes at room temperature.

fedoras

WHAT YOU WILL NEED:

Cake: To make 4 hats, bake 2 scant 6-inch rounds and 4 jumbo cupcakes of Pecan Cake (page 149)

Icing: Kaye's Buttercream (page 32); 12 ounces semisweet chocolate to make Chocolate Buttercream (page 33)

Decoration: ¼ cup dark wafer chocolate for accents, Chocolate Plastic (page 109) for ribbon (optional)

Tip: #45 flat tip (you can substitute a #104 petal tip)

Colors: red, yellow, and brown liquid gel colors

Miscellaneous: two 6-inch round pans, one 6-mold jumbo muffin pan, pastry bag, coupler, pastry cones, turntable, four 6-inch cardboard rounds, four 8-inch (or larger) bases

HOW TO

1. Bake the cakes and let them cool completely. Prepare the icing.

2. Prepare the flavored and tinted buttercream: 4 cups Chocolate Buttercream and (optional) ¼ cup dark chocolate buttercream (darken the chocolate by adding red, yellow, and brown liquid gel), 1 tablespoon yellow, 1 tablespoon white, 1 tablespoon red.

3. Cut the 6-inch round cakes horizontally into 2 equal layers. Cut the dome off of the cupcakes. Place each 6-inch round cake, crumb side down, onto a 6-inch cardboard or thick grease-proof paper round, adhering it with a dollop of buttercream. Cut a triangular section out of the top of each large muffin and discard or enjoy as a snack. Crumb-coat the cakes with some of the Chocolate Buttercream as directed on page 24.

4. Ice the cakes with a smooth finish (see page 28).

5. Place an iced 6-inch cake onto its base. Place a cupcake in the center of the 6-inch round.

6. To make a buttercream ribbon, place the dark brown buttercream into a pastry bag with a coupler, and with a #45 flat tip pipe a ribbon border around the base of the muffin. If you like, pipe vertical chocolate stripes on it to simulate grosgrain ribbon.

To make a ribbon of chocolate plastic, tint half of the plastic dark brown. Dust a clean, flat surface with cornstarch. With a rolling pin, roll out the plastic to ⅛ inch thick. Cut it into four ¾ x 10-inch strips. Score it with a knife's edge or fork edge repeatedly into the plastic to give the grosgrain effect. Place one end of the strip down on the cake starting at the base of the hat, carefully draping around until it meets itself. Using scissors, cut off any extra plastic.

7 Melt the dark wafer chocolate and pour it into a pastry cone. Place the red, white, and yellow buttercreams into separate pastry cones. Cut a small hole in the tip of each.

8 Pipe a feather coming out of the hat's ribbon using the chocolate and colored buttercream. Pipe one long white line. From this line pipe parallel lines at a 30-degree angle in red, yellow, chocolate, and white.

9 For fullest flavor, serve the cakes at room temperature.

baseball caps

Cake: To make 12 hats, bake 12 mini bowls of Pecan Cake (page 149)

Icing: Chocolate Glaze (page 34)

Decoration: 3 cups dark wafer chocolate to make 12 baseball cap brims, and ¼ cup white wafer chocolate for stitching

Miscellaneous: two 6-mold mini bowl pans, pastry cones, brim templates (page 170), 1 half-sheet pan, parchment paper or cellophane, twelve 6-inch (or larger) bases

HOW TO

1 Bake the cakes and let them cool completely. Cut the bottom dome off of the bowls, and freeze the cakes for at least 30 minutes. Prepare the Chocolate Glaze.

2 Melt the dark wafer and white wafer chocolates separately. Using the templates provided, make 12 brims as illustrated in The Chocolate Method (pages 40—43). Set aside to harden.

3 Glaze the tops of the cakes as directed in Chocolate Glaze on a Cake (page 29).

4 Invert the brim onto its base, adhering with a dot of glaze. With the help of a metal spatula, place the cap so that it overlaps the brim approximately ¼ inch.

5 Pipe stitching on the brim and hat with white chocolate.

6 For fullest flavor, serve the cakes at room temperature.

pecan cakes*

YIELD:
WITCH HATS: 4 witch hats
STRAW HATS: 6 straw hats
FEDORAS: 4 fedoras
BASEBALL CAPS: 12 caps

One of my favorite cakes at the Bakehouse is our hazelnut cake. We fine-tuned our recipe to achieve a lighter consistency and substituted my mom's favorite nut, the pecan. The result is a fragrant and delicious cake. If you don't want to fuss with decorating, for delicious redundancy simply buy a pint of butter pecan ice cream and serve the cupcakes à la mode.

For witch hats, grease two 6-inch round pans and one 4-mold mini cone pan.

For straw hats, grease three 6-inch round pans and one 6-mold mini bowl pan.

For fedoras, grease two 6-inch round pans and 4 molds of a 6-mold jumbo muffin pan.

For baseball hats, grease two 6-mold mini bowl pans.

Preheat the oven to 350°F. Have all ingredients at room temperature.

In the bowl of an electric mixer, beat at high speed until light and fluffy:
- 4 ounces (1 stick) unsalted butter
- 1½ cups brown sugar, packed

Add at medium speed and beat until well creamed:
- 2 large eggs
- 1 teaspoon pure vanilla extract

On a piece of wax paper, sift together:
- 2 cups cake flour
- ½ teaspoon salt
- ½ teaspoon baking powder
- 1 teaspoon baking soda

At low speed, add the dry ingredients to the butter mixture alternately with:
- 1 cup buttermilk

Beat the batter at medium-low speed until it is smooth, then stir in by hand:
- 1 cup finely chopped toasted pecans (see Note)

Pour the batter into the prepared pans.

Fill the mini bowl, mini cone, or jumbo muffin pans three-quarters full. Fill each 6-inch round with 1 cup of batter. Bake the bowl cakes for 12 to 18 minutes, or until a cake tester inserted into the center of a cake comes out clean. Bake the cone, jumbo muffin, and 6-inch round cakes for 20 to 25 minutes, or until a cake tester inserted into the center of a cake comes out clean. Cool on a wire rack for 15 to 20 minutes before turning the cakes out of the pans.

NOTE:

To toast pecans, place the nuts on an ungreased sheet pan. Bake at 350°F for 12 to 15 minutes, or until fragrant. Let cool.

3-d apple bushels**

*During my first couple of years as a cake decorator I would create a limited-*edition three-dimensional cake every week. In the fall I made these apple bushels and our customers loved them. We still make them every apple-picking season. The faux wood slats are created with variegated buttercream, and sweet buttercream apples overflow from the bushel.*

WHAT YOU WILL NEED:

Cake
16 jumbo Apple Cupcakes (see page 152)

Icing
3 recipes of Kaye's Buttercream (page 32); Dulce de Leche (page 101)

Decoration
1 cup dark wafer chocolate

Colors
red, brown, green, and yellow (optional) liquid gel colors

Tips
#45 flat tip (you can substitute a #104 petal tip), and a #45 leaf tip

Miscellaneous
3 jumbo muffin pans, pastry bag, coupler, pastry cones, turntable, sixteen 6-inch (or larger) bases

1. Bake the cupcakes and let them cool completely. Do not trim the domes off. Chill for 1 hour to overnight.

2. Prepare the buttercream. Set aside ¾ cup uncolored buttercream. Prepare the flavored and tinted buttercream: approximately 4 cups dulce de leche buttercream (3½ cups buttercream with ¾ cup plus 2 tablespoons dulce de leche), ½ cup dark brown, 4 cups red, and 1 cup green buttercream.

3. Place a dot of dulce de leche buttercream on the underside of each cake and place the cake in the center of its base.

4. With a metal spatula, spread a small strip of dark brown buttercream up one side of the interior of a pastry bag with a coupler. Spread a white strip up the opposite side. Fill the rest of the bag with dulce de leche buttercream. Place the cupcake and its base on a turntable, and with a # 45 flat tip pipe slats up the side of the cake. Keep the tip flush to the cake surface. Start piping each slat at the bottom of the cake and pipe to the top using a consistent pressure. Overlap each slat slightly so no cake will show through. Continue piping until you've covered the entire side of the cake with vertical slats. With a metal spatula, scrape off any excess buttercream that may have come over the top edge.

5. With the remaining variegated dulce de leche buttercream, pipe a rim around the outside top edge and around the center of each bushel.

6. With a spatula, spread a small strip of dark brown buttercream up one side of the interior of a pastry bag. Spread a white stripe up the opposite side. Fill the rest of the bag with red. Pipe one quarter-size apple "hemisphere" in the center of each bushel. Pipe an additional 6 apples around the center one.

7. Place the green buttercream into a pastry bag with a coupler, and with a leaf tip pipe leaves randomly around the top of the bushel.

8. Melt the dark wafer chocolate and pour it into a pastry cone. Cut a small hole in the pastry cone and pipe small nails randomly around the wood slats and pipe stems on the apples. Fill in the spaces between the apples with chocolate to give the effect of shadow.

9. For fullest flavor, serve the cakes at room temperature.

apple cupcakes*

The first incarnation of my mom's Apple Cake was really a cake, but nowadays you will most often find this treat disguising itself on the shelves of the Bakehouse as our apple muffin. If you are not up for the task of decorating a bunch of apple bushels, just whip up a batch of apple muffins instead. You can even slice them in half and serve with fresh Cinnamon Chocolate Whipped Cream (page 113).

Grease 16 molds of three 6-mold jumbo muffin pans. Preheat the oven to 350°F. Have all ingredients at room temperature.

In the bowl of an electric mixer, beat at high speed until light and fluffy:

- 1 cup vegetable oil
- 1 cup granulated sugar
- ¼ cup brown sugar, packed

Add and beat on medium speed until well creamed:

- 2 large eggs
- ½ teaspoon pure vanilla extract

On a piece of wax paper, sift together:

- 2 cups all-purpose flour
- 1½ teaspoons baking soda
- 1½ teaspoons ground cinnamon
- ½ teaspoon ground nutmeg
- ¼ teaspoon ground cloves
- 1 teaspoon salt

Mix the dry ingredients into the sugar and egg mixture at low speed just until combined.

Mix in:

- 2 cups Granny Smith apples, peeled, cored, and grated (from about 1½ apples)
- ½ to ¾ cup chopped toasted walnuts (see Note)

Pour the batter into the prepared molds, filling each mold three-quarters full. Bake for 25 to 30 minutes, or until a cake tester inserted into the center of a cupcake comes out clean. Cool on a wire rack for 15 to 20 minutes before turning the cakes out of the pans.

NOTE:

To toast walnuts, place the nuts on an ungreased sheet pan. Bake at 350°F for 12 to 15 minutes, or until fragrant. Let cool.

flower pots***

I've always wanted to make miniature flower pots. At the Bakehouse we make large (6-inch round by 8-inch tall) flower-pot cakes filled with African violets every Mother's Day. And for St. Patty's Day we fill the pot with golden wild roses (Flower-Pot-of-Gold). After a little brainstorming I decided I would try making the terra-cotta pots out of chocolate instead of cake and tinted buttercream. Three-ounce plastic cups became my mold. A delicious confection of Whipped Chocolate Ganache, cookie crumbs, and a Chocolate Butter Mini-Cupcake simulate the rich soil the buttercream violets sprout from.

WHAT YOU WILL NEED:

Cake
½ recipe of Chocolate Butter Cake (page 155) to make 50 cupcakes

Icing
House Buttercream (page 31) or Kaye's Buttercream (page 32)

Filling
Whipped Chocolate Ganache (page 105)

Decoration
2 ¼ cups dark wafer chocolate and 8 cups white wafer chocolate to make 50 chocolate shovels and flower pots; approximately ½ cup chocolate cookie crumbs (optional)

Colors
purple, green, and yellow liquid gel colors and orange candy color

Tips
#101 petal tip, #263 leaf tip

Miscellaneous
three mini muffin pans, pastry bag, coupler, pastry cones, shovel template (page 173), 1 half-sheet pan, parchment paper or cellophane, fifty 3-ounce plastic drinking cups, fifty 4-inch (or larger) bases

1. Prepare the chocolate ganache. Bake the cakes and let them cool completely. Freeze for 1 hour to overnight.

2. Prepare the buttercream.

3. Melt the dark wafer and white wafer chocolates separately. Mix 3⅛ cups white chocolate with a generous ¼ cup dark chocolate. Add orange candy color drop by drop until you have a terra-cotta color. Using the Color Mixing Chart on pages 44–45, tint the remaining white chocolate gray. Using the template provided, make 50 shovels as illustrated in The Chocolate Method (pages 40–43). Set aside to harden.

4. Cut fifty 3-ounce plastic cups down one side to the base. Tape the slit closed. Pour approximately 2 tablespoons of "terra cotta" into each cup. With a small metal spatula, spread the chocolate so that it covers the entire interior surface of the cup as evenly as possible. Invert the cup onto a wire rack over parchment paper. Let the chocolate drip and set for 3 to 5 minutes. Turn the cups right side up and with a small knife scrape any extra chocolate off the top edge. Place the cups in the freezer for 3 to 5 minutes or just until hard.

5. Remove the cups from the freezer. Remove the tape from the side of the cup. Carefully pull the cup away from the chocolate and remove the pots. Set aside.

6. Whip the chocolate ganache. Remove the cupcakes from the freezer.

7. Place the whipped ganache into a pastry bag with a coupler. Pipe a dollop of ganache in the bottom of each terra-cotta cup. If desired, sprinkle some chocolate cookie crumbs on top (approximately ½ teaspoon per pot) and then pipe more ganache until it reaches two thirds of the way to the top edge. Place one cupcake on the top. The bottom of the cupcake should touch the ganache, and the top of it should slightly rise above the terra-cotta cup.

8. Prepare the colored buttercream: approximately 2 cups violet, 1¼ cups green, and 3 tablespoons yellow buttercream.

9. Place the violet buttercream into a pastry bag with a coupler, and with the #101 tip pipe 1 violet in the center and 5 to 6 violets around the center one. To pipe violets refer to the directions for piping hydrangea on page 133 with one difference: instead of 4 petals, the violet has 5 petals.

10. Place the green buttercream into a pastry bag with a coupler, and with the #263 tip pipe leaves in the empty spaces between the flowers.

11. Place the yellow buttercream into a pastry cone and cut a small hole in the tip. Pipe two yellow dots in the center of each flower.

12. Plate the pots with the shovel at their side. If you are traveling, adhere the pots to a cardboard base with a large dot of melted chocolate; hold in place until set. For an added effect, scoop some chocolate ganache onto the shovel and dip it in chocolate cookie crumbs, and/or spread some chocolate ganache on the base and encrust with cookie crumbs.

13. For fullest flavor, serve the cakes at room temperature.

chocolate butter cake
or mini cupcakes*

YIELD: TWO 3-TIERED (2-INCH, 3-INCH, AND 4-INCH)
CAKES OR 100 MINI CUPCAKES

This has to be our best cake. We've been baking this amazing recipe for more than twenty years. Take care not to discard the dome of the cake; devour it without shame! It's the moistest and most delicious part.

This recipe does not bake well in standard cupcake molds unless the molds are nonstick Teflon, because even when greased, the tops of the cupcake tend to stick to the top of the pan. However, we had no problems with the mini cupcake pans or other pans if greased and floured.

For tiered cakes, grease and flour two 2-inch, two 3-inch, and two 4-inch round cake pans.

For Flower Pots, cut this recipe in half and grease and flour two 24-mold mini muffin pans plus 2 more molds. Preheat the oven to 350°F. Have all ingredients at room temperature.

In a small bowl, combine:
- ½ cup hot coffee
- ½ cup cocoa powder

Whisk until there are no lumps.

Add and whisk until smooth:
- ½ cup cold water

On a piece of wax paper, sift together:
- 1½ cups cake flour
- 1 teaspoon baking soda
- ¼ teaspoon baking powder
- ¼ teaspoon salt

In the bowl of an electric mixer, beat at high speed until light and fluffy:
- 4 ounces (1 stick) unsalted butter
- 1¼ cups sugar

On medium speed, add slowly and cream well:
- 2 large eggs
- ¾ teaspoon pure vanilla extract

Add the flour mixture to the egg mixture alternately with the cocoa, mixing until smooth.

Scoop the batter into the molds: The 2-inch round uses a scant ¼ cup of batter, the 3-inch round uses a generous ½ cup of batter, and the 4-inch round uses 1 cup of batter. Each mini muffin mold will hold 1 tablespoon of batter. Bake the 4-inch for 20 to 25 minutes, the 3-inch for 20 to 22 minutes, the 2-inch for 15 to 18 minutes, and the mini cupcakes for 12 to 14 minutes. Cool on a wire rack for 15 minutes before turning them out of their pans.

3-d christmas trees **

Every Christmas we make a limited edition of these cakes, but about 6 inches taller. Strung with lights and decorated with festive ornaments and wrapped presents, they will add to the merry atmosphere when placed on your holiday table. Or, instead of a gingerbread house or fruit cake, make these trees as gifts to share with your friends and family.

WHAT YOU WILL NEED:

Cake
6 gingerbread mini cone cakes (see page 158)

Icing
1½ recipes Kaye's Buttercream (page 32)

Filling
Eggnog Cream (page 159; optional)

Decoration
½ cup dark wafer chocolate and 3 cups white wafer chocolate to make doves, stars, bears, rocking horses, candy canes, bulbs, and presents, and ¼ cup edible gel for a garland

Colors
green, blue, and yellow liquid gel colors; and red, yellow, blue, purple, and pink candy colors

Tip
#133 multi-opening tip (you can substitute a #233 tip)

Miscellaneous
two 4-mold mini cone pans, pastry bag, coupler, pastry cones, decoration templates (page 169), 1 half-sheet pan, parchment paper or cellophane, turntable, six 6-inch (or larger) bases

1. Bake the cakes and let them cool completely. Prepare the buttercream.

2. If desired, prepare the filling. To fill the cake, cut each cone in half horizontally and with a small paring knife cut out a 2-inch-long by ¾-inch-deep cone from the bottom of the cake and a 1-inch-long by ¾-inch-deep cone from the top. Fill the holes with a generous amount of eggnog cream and replace the top on the cone. Gently push down on the cake allowing some of the cream to seep out, adhering the two sides. Scrape off any cream that may have come through the seam. Chill for 30 minutes.

3. Melt the dark wafer and white wafer chocolates separately. Set aside 2 tablespoons white chocolate. Using the Color Mixing Chart on pages 44—45, tint the remaining white chocolate: approximately 2 tablespoons each of dark blue, light blue, pink, orange, yellow, red, light green, green, violet, light brown, dark brown. Using the templates provided, make approximately 30 each of the bulbs, stars, bears, rocking horses, and candy canes. Also make 6 of each present and 6 larger stars to top the trees, as illustrated in The Chocolate Method (pages 40—43). Set aside to harden.

4. Prepare the tinted buttercream: approximately ¼ cup yellow and 5¾ cups green. In addition mix 2 drops of yellow liquid-gel color with ¼ cup of clear piping gel.

5. Adhere the cake to its base with a dollop of green buttercream. Place the cake and base on a turntable.

6. Place the green buttercream into a pastry bag with a coupler. Pipe a large point (much like a Hershey's kiss) on top of the cone. Place a #133 tip on the pastry bag and pipe out pine needles as follows: Place the tip ¼ inch from the base, squeeze, and pull downward at a 45-degree angle. Release the pressure when the pine needles are about ½ inch long. Go around the entire base in this manner. Start the next row directly above the last row; the bottom of the tip touches the top edge of the first row. Continue piping overlapping rows. As you get closer to the top, the angle of the tip will change from 45 degrees downward to level to 45 degrees upward. The last row is just one stroke straight up.

7. Place the yellow buttercream and yellow gel into separate pastry cones and cut a small hole into the tip of each. To create a garland, pipe a continuous line of small yellow dots spiraling up and around the cake, then back down again, crisscrossing itself. Pipe swags of gel around the tree.

8. Place the ornaments randomly around the cake and a star on top. Place the presents at the base of the cake.

9. For fullest flavor, serve the cakes at room temperature.

gingerbread cakes*

YIELD: 6 CONES

Gingerbread isn't just a cookie, it also manifests itself as a delicious cake; in fact, this was one of our home testers' favorite recipes. You can bake it in a loaf pan, slice, and serve with Eggnog Cream or go for broke and make a spectacular Christmas tree as on page 156.

Grease 6 molds of two 4-mold mini cone pans. Preheat the oven to 350°F. Have all ingredients at room temperature.

In the bowl of an electric mixer, beat at high speed until light and fluffy:
- 4 ounces (1 stick) unsalted butter
- ¾ cup sugar
- ½ cup molasses

Add at medium speed and beat until well creamed:
- 1 large egg

On a piece of wax paper, sift together:
- 2 cups all-purpose flour
- 1 teaspoon baking soda
- 2 teaspoons ground ginger
- ½ teaspoon ground nutmeg
- 1 teaspoon ground cinnamon
- ¼ teaspoon ground cloves
- ½ teaspoon salt

At low speed, add the dry ingredients to the butter mixture alternately with:
- 1 cup milk

Fold in:
- ¼ cup minced crystallized ginger

Divide the batter evenly among the 6 cones. Bake for 18 to 22 minutes or until a cake tester inserted into the center of a cake comes out clean. Cool the cakes on a wire rack for 5 minutes before turning them out of their pans.

eggnog cream *

This classic yuletide flavor when paired with whipped cream is a perfect accompaniment to our Gingerbread Cake, but it is also great spooned into your evening coffee.

For best results, we recommend preparing the cream right before serving or assembling your cakes. Any leftovers can be stored in an airtight container in the refrigerator for up to 3 days. The cream will break down as it sits in the refrigerator, so rewhip in the bowl of an electric mixer for 1 minute or until medium to stiff peaks form.

In the bowl of an electric mixer fitted with a whisk attachment, whip until stiff:
- 1¼ cups heavy cream
- ¼ cup confectioners' sugar
- 1 teaspoon pure vanilla extract
- Dash of nutmeg (or to taste)

tiered mini cakes***

Instead of making a grandiose statement by having a large tiered cake at their wedding receptions, some brides and grooms are opting for a collection of tiered miniature cakes to present to each table or each guest. These little versions of the classic can be just as traditional in their appearance as their larger cousins, or they can take a turn for the whimsical with bright fun palettes and carefree designs.

Of course a tiered cake isn't just for weddings anymore. We make just as many for birthdays. Make an individual tiered cake for that special someone, and let the rest of the party guests eat a regular cake.

Here are three takes on the tiered mini cake: Mariana's Paisley (inspired by a former colleague's cake doodles), Lovely Lilacs, and Dragon Cake.

mariana's paisley

WHAT YOU WILL NEED:

Cake: **Two 3-tiered Chocolate Butter Cakes (each of which has a 2-inch, 3-inch, and 4-inch round layer) (page 155)**

Filling: **Apricot Mousse (page 167)**

Icing: **Kaye's Buttercream (page 32)**

Colors: **yellow, green, orange, neon pink, and violet liquid gel colors**

Miscellaneous: **Two 2-inch, 3-inch, and 4-inch round pans; two each 2-inch, 3-inch, and 4-inch cardboard rounds; pastry bag; coupler; pastry cones; turntable; drinking straws; two sturdy serving plates or bases at least 3 inches larger than the bottom tier**

HOW TO

1. Bake the cakes and let them cool completely. Prepare the icing and filling. Place the cakes on cardboard rounds of the same diameter. Fill and crumb-coat each individual cake as illustrated in Filling (page 23) and Crumbing (page 24). You will need approximately 1½ cups of filling and 1½ cups of buttercream for crumbing all of the round tiers. Chill the filled cakes for an hour.

2. Set aside ¼ cup uncolored buttercream. Prepare the colored buttercream: approximately 2 cups yellow, 2 tablespoons pale orange, 2 tablespoons coral, 2 tablespoons dark coral, 2 tablespoons pale neon green.

3. Ice the cakes with a flat finish (page 26) of yellow buttercream.

4. Place a dot of glue on the center of each base and adhere the two bottom (4-inch) tiers to them.

5. In the center of each bottom tier, press a straw all the way into the center of the cake. (Ideally the cake is level and all points are the same height.) Mark the straw at the buttercream line with a pen or hold it with your finger. You'll use this to create straws that will support the cake. Remove the straw and cut it ¹⁄₁₆ inch shorter than that line, using scissors. Using this straw as a guide, cut 2 to 4 more straws to the same length. Insert the straws into the cakes, evenly spaced within the area over which the next tier will be placed. Pipe a small dot of buttercream on top of each straw.

6. Center the second (3-inch) tiers on top of the bottom tiers. Cut 1 straw support for each cake (see step 5) and insert them into the center of each cake. Pipe a small dot of buttercream on top of the straws.

7. Center the third (2-inch) tiers on top of the second tiers.

8. Place the remaining colored buttercream into separate pastry cones. Cut small to medium holes in the tip of each. Pipe a dot border on the bottom of each tier (see below for piping dots). Pipe colorful paisley and/or filigree patterns all over the tiers (see below for piping filigree). Use the photograph as a guide, or make up your own pattern.

9. For fullest flavor, serve the cakes at room temperature.

DOTS

Tips: #2 to #12 round tip or pastry cone

Hold the bag perpendicular to the cake surface. Keeping the tip stationary, apply consistent pressure until the dot is the desired size. Release the pressure and tail off gently to the side or in a spiral to give a rounded finish.

LINES AND FILIGREE

Tips: #2 to #7 round tip or a pastry cone

Hold the bag at a 45-degree angle to the cake surface. Touch the tip to the surface where you want to begin piping, then lift the tip up as you begin to apply pressure and move the pastry bag in the desired direction. To end the line, touch the tip to the surface of the cake again and discontinue the pressure.

lovely lilacs

WHAT YOU WILL NEED:

Cake: Two 3-tiered Chocolate Butter Cakes (each of which has a 2-inch, 3-inch, and 4-inch round layer) (page 155)

Filling: Apricot Mousse (page 167)

Icing: Kaye's Buttercream (page 32)

Tips: #2 or 3 round tip, #263 leaf tip, #44 or 45 flat tip

Colors: green, brown, and violet liquid gel colors

Miscellaneous: Two 2-inch, 3-inch, and 4-inch round pans; two each 2-inch, 3-inch, and 4-inch cardboard rounds; pastry bag; coupler; pastry cones; turntable; drinking straws; two sturdy serving plates or bases at least 3 inches larger than the bottom tier

1. Bake the cakes and let them cool completely. Prepare the icing and filling. Place the cakes on cardboard rounds of the same diameter. Fill and crumb-coat each individual cake as illustrated in Filling (page 23) and Crumbing (page 24). You will need approximately 1½ cups of filling and 1½ cups of buttercream for crumbing all of the round tiers. Chill the filled cakes for an hour.

2. Ice the cakes with a flat finish (page 26) of plain white buttercream. Adhere the cardboard rounds supporting the bottom (4-inch) tiers to their bases.

3. To assemble the tiers, follow steps 5, 6, and 7 of Mariana's Paisley (page 161).

4. Place the buttercream into a pastry bag with a coupler, and with the #45 tip pipe a flat ribbon border (see below) around the base of each tier.

5. Prepare the colored buttercream: approximately ¼ cup pale violet, scant ¼ cup violet, 2 tablespoons dark brown, ¼ cup green.

6. Place the brown buttercream into a pastry cone and cut a small hole in the tip. Pipe a branch running up the side of the tiers. The branch should have smaller stems that shoot off it. These stems should have an overall conical form, since on a real tree the stems get fewer and narrower as they grow.

7. With a metal spatula, spread a stripe of light violet up one side of a pastry bag with a coupler. Fill the rest of the bag with violet. With a #2 or 3 round tip pipe small teardrops starting at the outer edges of the branches and pulling in toward the center stem. The petals should be fuller the closer you get to the center stem. Fill in the center of the lilac with dots and add a few 4-petal teardrop blossoms to complete the flower.

8. Place the green buttercream into a pastry bag with a coupler and with a #263 leaf tip pipe leaves sporadically around the lilacs.

9. For fullest flavor, serve the cakes at room temperature.

FLAT RIBBON BORDER

Tips: #44 or 45 flat tip

Hold the bag at a 45-degree angle to the cake surface. With the wide end of the tip down, apply consistent pressure while piping a ribbon flush to the cake surface. Keep the narrow end lightly brushing the surface of the cake to ensure that it adheres.

dragon cake

WHAT YOU WILL NEED:

Cake: Celebration Cake (page 166)

Filling and Icing: Kaye's Buttercream (page 32), Praline Powder (page 167), and 1½ ounces chopped semisweet chocolate to make flavored buttercream

Decoration: ¼ cup dark wafer chocolate and 2½ cups white chocolate to make the dragon's face, scales, legs, and polka dots

Colors: pink and green liquid gel colors and red, orange, yellow, green, blue, violet, and neon pink candy colors

Miscellaneous: Two half-sheet pans; pastry cones; 5-inch and 3-inch square cardboards; dragon templates (page 168); parchment paper or cellophane; turntable; drinking straws; sturdy serving plate or base at least 3 inches larger than the bottom tier

HOW TO

1. Prepare the Praline Powder. Bake the cakes and let them cool completely. Prepare the buttercream. Prepare the flavored buttercream for the filling. To make the praline buttercream, combine 1 cup buttercream and ⅓ cup praline powder. To make the chocolate buttercream, combine 1½ ounces chocolate, melted and allowed to cool to body temperature, and ½ cup buttercream.

2. Cut the cakes as directed in the recipe. Stack the 5-inch cake layers on the 5-inch cardboard square and the 3-inch cake layers on the 3-inch cardboard square. Fill and crumb-coat each individual cake as illustrated in Filling (page 23) and Crumbing (page 24) using praline buttercream between the bottom 2 layers, chocolate buttercream on top of the second layer, and another layer of praline buttercream between the top layers. Each tier will have 4 layers of cake, 2 layers of praline buttercream, and 1 layer of chocolate buttercream. Chill the filled cakes for 1 hour.

3. Melt the dark wafer and white wafer chocolates separately. Reserve 1 tablespoon white chocolate. Tint the remaining white chocolate: approximately ¼ cup neon green, 2 tablespoons teal, 2 tablespoons violet, 2 tablespoons orange, 2 tablespoons yellow, 2 tablespoons red, 2 tablespoons green, 2 tablespoons neon pink. Using the templates provided, trace two dragon heads onto parchment paper. Turn one upside down and one right side up. Place another piece of parchment over them. Make the two dragon heads, plus 4 feet,

multicolored teardrop-shaped scales, spikes, and pink and green polka dots as illustrated in The Chocolate Method (pages 40–43). Set aside to harden.

4. Prepare the colored buttercream: approximately 1½ cups light green and ½ cup pale pink. Reserve approximately 1 tablespoon of each color and tint it one shade darker. Place the darker colors into separate pastry bags.

5. Ice the cakes with a flat finish (page 27), the bottom tier in green and the top tier in pink. Pipe pinpoint dots on the tiers in the same hue as the icing. Adhere the cardboard squares supporting the bottom (5-inch) tier to its base.

6. In the center of the bottom tier, press a straw all the way into the center of the cake. (Ideally the cake is level and all points are the same height.) Mark the straw at the buttercream line with a pen or hold it with your finger. You'll use this to create straws that will support the cake. Remove the straw and cut it 1⁄16 inch shorter than that line, using scissors. Using this straw as a guide, cut 4 more straws to the same length. Insert the straws into the cake, evenly spaced within the area over which the next tier will be placed. Pipe a small dot of buttercream on top of each straw.

7. Stack the top tier so that it is kitty-corner to the bottom tier.

8. Stick the pink chocolate polka dots to the bottom border of the pink cake and the green chocolate polka dots to the bottom border of the green cake.

9. Mark where the dragon head will be on the side of the top tier. It should come up over the top edge approximately 2 inches. Line up the other head so that it will be directly behind the first head, ½ to ¾ inch away, with the back or underside facing the front. With a sharp knife, score the top of the cake where it will be inserted. Slowly and carefully press the dragon head into the cake, until it lines up directly behind the other. Place any leftover green buttercream in a pastry bag with a coupler. Pipe buttercream on the back side of the dragon, then stick the forward-facing dragon head into the buttercream directly in front of the inserted head.

10. Pipe an undulating line from the dragon's neck down to the bottom tier, tailing off before you reach the base.

11. Place the spikes into the buttercream between the heads.

12. Starting at the bottom, stick the scales onto the buttercream (the points face upward). Overlap the rows, and offset them, so the points are disguised (refer to the photograph). Continue until you reach the dragon's neck and have covered all of the buttercream.

13. Stick the legs into the side of the dragon (refer to the photograph).

14. For fullest flavor, serve the cakes at room temperature.

celebration cake**

My mom has been making this cake since I was a child and I always loved to eat the scraps she trimmed off. I was so enamored of this unique cake that, for my fifth-grade French class, I entered it in a language fair baking contest at a local college. Suffice it to say, it won!

Grease and flour a half-sheet pan. Preheat the oven to 350°F. Have all ingredients at room temperature.

In a food processor, combine and finely chop:

- 6 ounces (1½ cups) toasted hazelnuts (see Note)
- 5 ounces (1 cup) toasted whole almonds (see Note)
- ¼ cup all-purpose flour

Transfer to a bowl and add:

- ¾ cup sugar

In the bowl of an electric mixer at medium speed, use a whip attachment to beat until frothy:

- 1¼ cups egg whites (from 10 to 12 eggs)
- ½ teaspoon cream of tartar
- ¼ teaspoon salt

Continue beating at high speed while gradually adding:

- ¼ cup sugar

Beat until very stiff.

Fold in the nut mixture.

Pour the batter into the prepared pan. Using an offset spatula, spread the batter evenly onto the sheet pan. Bake for 17 to 22 minutes, or until golden brown. Cool the cake in its pan on a wire rack. Using an offset spatula, loosen the edges and bottom of the cake from the pan. To make the tiered Dragon Cake on page 164 cut the cooled cake as follows: Measuring the horizontal (or 16-inch) side of the cake with a ruler, lightly score the cake into two 5-inch strips and two 3-inch strips. From these strips cut out four 5-inch squares and four 3-inch squares (you will have extra 3-inch squares and 2 x 5-inch strips). To fill and assemble the cakes follow the Dragon Cake directions.

To assemble and ice a plain Celebration Cake cut the cake into four 6 x 8-inch pieces. Stack the layers on a 6 x 8-inch piece of cardboard. Prepare 2 cups of praline buttercream and 2 cups of chocolate buttercream. Fill the cake with 2 layers of praline buttercream and 1 layer of chocolate buttercream as described in Filling a Cake (page 23). Spread a thin layer of chocolate buttercream onto the sides of the cake and press on chopped nuts into the buttercream (approximately 1 cup). Dust the top with powdered sugar.

NOTE:

To toast the hazelnuts and almonds, place the nuts on an ungreased sheet pan. Bake at 350°F for 12 to 15 minutes or until fragrant. Let cool.

praline powder *

We use this recipe to flavor our praline buttercream, but we recommend topping your ice cream with this delicious concoction, too. Feel free to add your favorite nut in place of almonds.

In a small saucepan, bring to a boil:
- ½ cup sugar
- 2 tablespoons water

Dip a clean pastry brush in cold water and wash down the sugar crystals that form on the sides of the pot. Continue boiling on high heat until caramelized or the mixture has become a nut-brown color, about 7 minutes. Do not stir. If the sugar mixture colors unevenly, shake the pan. Take care, as this sugar mixture gets very hot.

Remove from the heat and stir in:
- ½ cup sliced almonds

Immediately pour onto a sheet pan lined with parchment paper or a silicone mat and let cool completely.

Break the praline into pieces and place into a food processor. Process until fine.

apricot mousse *

YIELD: 1½ CUPS

A little tang and a lot of yumminess. For best results, we recommend preparing the Apricot Mousse right before serving or assembling your cakes.

In the bowl of an electric mixer fitted with a whisk attachment, whip until stiff:
- ¾ cup heavy cream
- 3 tablespoons confectioners' sugar
- ½ teaspoon pure vanilla extract

In a small bowl, stir until smooth:
- Scant ¼ cup apricot jam

Gently fold the jam into the whipped cream.

t e m p l a t e s

To achieve the correct size for your little cakes, each
of the templates should be increased to four times
their size, or by 400 percent on your photocopier.

DRAGON CAKE (PAGES 164—165)

3-D CHRISTMAS TREES (PAGES 156—157)

SPIDERS (PAGES 122—123)

LADYBUGS (PAGES 122—123)

BE MINE CAKES (PAGES 110—111)

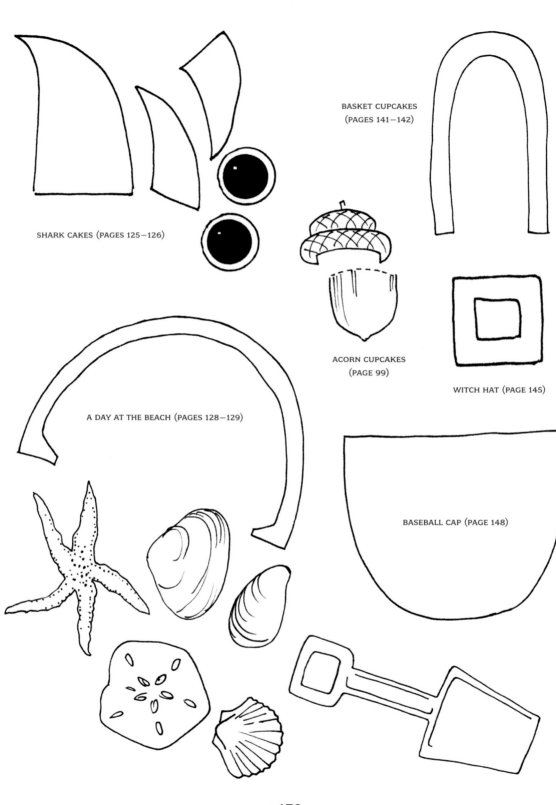

BASKET CUPCAKES
(PAGES 141–142)

SHARK CAKES (PAGES 125–126)

ACORN CUPCAKES
(PAGE 99)

WITCH HAT (PAGE 145)

A DAY AT THE BEACH (PAGES 128–129)

BASEBALL CAP (PAGE 148)

HALLOWEEN CUPCAKES (PAGES 96—97)

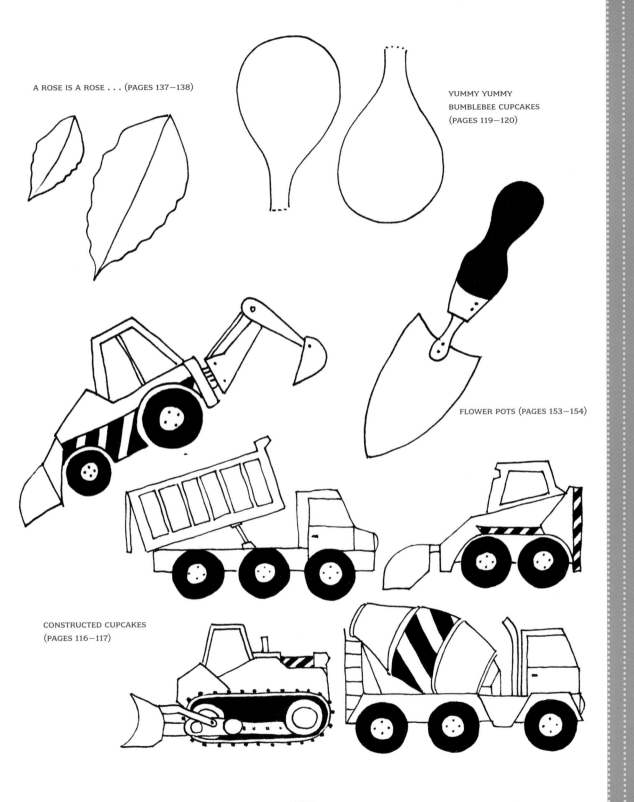

A ROSE IS A ROSE . . . (PAGES 137—138)

YUMMY YUMMY
BUMBLEBEE CUPCAKES
(PAGES 119—120)

FLOWER POTS (PAGES 153—154)

CONSTRUCTED CUPCAKES
(PAGES 116—117)

list of suppliers

The suppliers listed below stock baking and decorating tools
and ingredients that are not readily available in supermarkets.

WILLIAMS-SONOMA
Retail locations throughout the United States
877-812-6235
www.williams-sonoma.com

*In addition to carrying a wide range of bakeware
(including many of the pans used in this book)
and many specialty baking ingredients, this
national chain also carries great decorating
starter kits.*

WILTON INDUSTRIES, INC.
2240 West 75th St.
Woodridge, IL 60517
800-794-5866
www.wilton.com

*Decorating tools, bakeware, display equipment,
wafer chocolate, and food coloring.*

**NEW YORK CAKE AND BAKING
DISTRIBUTORS, INC.**
56 West 22nd St.
New York, NY 10010
Phone: 800-942-2539 or 212-675-7955

*Decorating supplies including food coloring,
pastry bags, and tips.*

**KING ARTHUR FLOUR BAKER'S
CATALOGUE**
58 Billings Farm Road
White River Junction, VT 05001
800-827-6836

Flagship Store:
135 Route 5 South
Norwich, VT 05055-0876
802-649-3361
www.kingarthurflour.com

*Everything from cake pans to electric mixers,
specialty ingredients to chocolate, decorating
tools, and display equipment.*

NORDIC WARE
www.nordicware.com

*This is the source for a wide range of bakeware,
including Bundt pans, unique mini shaped pans,
muffin tins, and much more. Check it out.*

THE FOODCRAFTER'S SUPPLY CATALOG
P.O. Box 442-OKD
Waukon, IA 52172-0442
800-776-0575
www.kitchenkrafts.com

*A wide range of baking and decorating tools
from candy-making equipment to bakeware and
display.*

PFEIL AND HOLING
58-15 Northern Blvd.
Woodside, NY 11377
Phone: 800-247-7955
www.cakedeco.com

*This is where the Bakehouse purchases the
majority of our decorating tools and colors.*

index Note: Page numbers in *italics* refer to illustrations